Relentless and Unbeatable

No Obstacle Is Too Extreme. All It Takes Is Old School Grit and A Hardened Mind.
You Can Achieve the Impossible with Mental Toughness

Eric H. Mennell

© Copyright 2019 - All rights reserved.

The content contained within this book may not be reproduced, duplicated or transmitted without direct written permission from the author or the publisher.

Under no circumstances will any blame or legal responsibility be held against the publisher, or author, for any damages, reparation, or monetary loss due to the information contained within this book. Either directly or indirectly.

Legal Notice:

This book is copyright protected. This book is only for personal use. You cannot amend, distribute, sell, use, quote or paraphrase any part, or the content within this book, without the consent of the author or publisher.

Disclaimer Notice:

Please note the information contained within this document is for educational and entertainment purposes only. All effort has been executed to present accurate, up to date, and reliable, complete information. No warranties of any kind are declared or implied. Readers acknowledge that the author is not engaging in the rendering of legal, financial, medical or professional advice. The content within this book has been derived from various sources. Please consult a licensed professional before attempting any techniques outlined in this book.

By reading this document, the reader agrees that under no circumstances is the author responsible for any losses, direct or indirect, which are incurred as a result of the use of information contained within this document, including, but not limited to, — errors, omissions, or inaccuracies.

Contents

Introduction _____ 1

Chapter 1:
An Unbeatable Mind _____ 3

Chapter 2:
The Right Attitude is a Must _____ 11

Chapter 3:
A Navy SEAL'S Mindset _____ 18

Chapter 4:
Simple Yet Effective Strategies to Strengthen the Mind _____ 28

Chapter 5:
From Fragile to a Champions Mind _____ 32

Chapter 6:
The Hidden Rule to Push Yourself to the Limit _____ 45

Chapter 7:
How to Create Confidence when Humiliated _____ 58

Chapter 8:
How Navy SEALS Stay in Control in Any Situation _____ 68

Chapter 9:
How the Extraordinary Stay Extraordinary _____ 82

Chapter 10:
Anti-Habits Holding You Back from Your True Potential _____ 96

Chapter 11:
Why Losers Never Get Better _____ 104

Chapter 12:
Forge an Unrelentless Mind and Never Stay Down _____ 119

Conclusion _____ 127

Introduction

Have you ever wondered what makes some people stand out and seem so unstoppable? Why do some people seem to always have things going well, and everything working in their favor?

These are not extraordinary men with special abilities. These are men that have identified limitations and everything that could be a clog in the wheel of progress. They are neither from Mars or an alternate planet. They have identified their obstacles and faced them head-on. They do not get knocked down by anything that happens to them and has developed themselves in a way that nothing can deter them.

- Have you ever wondered what these kinds of people are made of?

- What is the source of their passion and motivation?

- What keeps them going despite all odds?

- How did they get so tough that they are able to overcome the limitations of the mind?

It's no miracle, nor is there anything special that sets these people apart. These are simply people that have learned to get around the mental barrier and limitations of their mind. They possess a relentless drive to get around every obstacle set in their path. They face a task and approach it with a can-do attitude, no matter how difficult it is.

These types of people did not become like this overnight. They did not just overcome the mental barrier in a day, neither did they get their mind to stop seeing impossibilities just like that. This happened as a result of a series of effective strategies and techniques to reconfigure their mindset.

This is what this book plans to offer you. In this life-changing manual are tips, tactics, and strategies to build your mental strength. With this book, no task will ever freak you out again and the impossible will be deleted from your dictionary.

To everyone out there ready to bring out the best in themselves and set daring goals and face them head-on, you will find this book very helpful.

With cognitive behavioral therapy, you can completely alter your mindset and become a fearless person who sees possibility in everything.

Chapter 1:
An Unbeatable Mind

Many times, humans are faced with certain problems that may seem insurmountable and the nature of man, which seems to possess many weaknesses, will not always serve as a guide if he does not rely on the strengths that are within him. Therefore, relying solely on these weaknesses only places one on the path to failure. Although a person might have set out to achieve success at all cost, situations or conditions may not favor the goals that they have set out to achieve. These conditions come in different shapes and forms of barriers and stumbling blocks. However, one cannot just pretend that these barriers are not real. The truth is, they are as real as they come and if not faced with caution, can bring a whole year or even a decade's effort to futility. In all cases, the first thing to note is the fact that these barriers are only physical, and it only goes to explain why they are so prominent. However, inside of you is a strong weapon that can break every barrier and chain - your mind.

To begin, let's try to pin a definition or maybe a face, to the mind. It is often described by experts as the core of everyone's existence. The mind is the seat of every human's wisdom as well as the center of one's consciousness. A person without a mind may as well be considered non-existent. According to scientists, the mind is the product of activities of the brain. While the brain is the physical property, the mind is the product of those active senses. However, recent research has proved that the mind isn't merely the physical activities of the brain; it goes way beyond that. Although the brain plays a very important role in the workings of the mind, it can't be confined to a compartment of the skull or even the entire body. According to extensive research by scientists, the mind is not just our perception of experiences, but the experiences itself. It is said that one cannot separate the subjective view of humans' perception of the world from his interaction with the world. Therefore, this brings us to the point where the mind is meant to control the activities of a man with his world, no matter the possibilities and impossibilities, constraints, and barriers. Certainly, the demands of everyday living may be so tasking that sometimes, they may seem impossible to surmount. In hard times, the only way to get above these situations is to put one's mind to work. You may wonder how that is possible if the mind is already preoccupied, if not weighed down with thoughts of what could have been and what isn't. The first step to breaking through, however, is to realize that these things only exist in your brain and in the physical. Once you realize this, you will find out that there is an endless scope of what you can achieve in your mind. You may want to imagine why people tend to give up on things easily when they feel like they have easier options, like, 'how do you expect me to stay up for three hours studying, when I can split my study hours between different days, especially when I do not have a deadline to meet?' Sometimes, it feels impossible to stay awake once you pick a book or sit down to write a term paper. When deadlines begin to stare us in the face, these impossibilities disappear completely. Suddenly, someone that could not initially focus for three hours can now go for five hours without even blinking. The fear of dropping from an 'A' to 'F' suddenly keeps you on your toes and makes you go to lengths that you previously considered impossible. This goes to show that sleepiness, time, and everything that served as a limitation was merely a product of the physical world, and they have nothing on your mind. Once you set your mind to it, you can achieve it. The following are ways the mind can turn limitations to possibilities.

Limitations Can Bring Out Your Creative Side

Do you remember the saying; necessity is the father of invention? Here's how it works: once you are faced with a tedious task that seems impossible, there may be only two ways out; to quit or to keep moving. If you quit, it was never so important to you, so you keep moving even though it seems impossible and to an outsider, you look like another joker on the path to failure. At this point, if you have chosen success, your mind automatically sets itself to look for ways to succeed. It is like you have been pushed to the wall and you now must fight back to liberate yourself. Such is the story of a certain young screenwriter, whose reputation seems to be on the line, as he is faced with the challenge of providing his viewers with equally interesting new episodes to his soap opera, which has since become an all-time favorite. Having added very interesting twists to his story, the life of his main character, who is the kernel of the show, is cut short as he dies in a fatal car crash. The writer now must decide if the show will die with the main character or not. In the mind of others, this might seem like a great limitation to the show, but it is at this point that the creativity of the writer will have to come into play. Ordinarily, this may be a dead end, but the limitation posed by the death of one character may be a push for a new/fresh start if the writer puts his creative mind to work. The possibilities are endless; all he needs is to tap into them. The physical limitations you see might just be the push you need to be more creative. Instead of listening to the voices in your head, it is always better to trust your mind and explore all the chances it creates.

The Central Governor Theory Versus the Placebo Effect

There is a theory that states that a part of a human's brain controls the energy supply and shuts the body down as a protective measure so that no permanent harm will come to it. This part of the body is called the central government and this theory claims that this governor has a conservative nature, so it sends pain signals to the body, making it seem as though it cannot take more pain way earlier than the body needs it. This is as a form of protection for the body to get some rest before the supply of energy is completely exhausted. Once

Relentless and Unbeatable

this central governor sends its signal, one is meant to think that he cannot go further and is therefore compelled to shut down and take some rest. The catch here is that the point when you are given this signal isn't the point when you are exhausted. Therefore, it takes determination to beat this signal and go further. This is only made possible by the mind.

Let's take the example of a kid that was made to run a marathon with much bigger kids at his school's sports competition. Once the race started, he seemed to be lagging and he soon began to feel exhausted. Not even the loud cheers from the crowd could propel him to go further. This is because the central government has already told him that he cannot go further and the gap between him and his bigger competitors doesn't seem to be helping either. Obviously, he isn't going to make it anywhere close to the top, so he would rather just quit. From the sideline, however, he is handed an energy drink and he gulp it with enthusiasm. Hopefully, the drink will be able to boost his strength. Surprisingly, he begins to get more energy and like magic, he starts closing in on the wide gap between himself and the closest person to him. He starts to pass more people than he could ever have imagined and as it was down to the last lap, it became obvious that he was going to finish well. He ended up finishing amongst the top three and that was a great achievement for him as he didn't appear to be as big as the rest of the kids in the race. If he was to thank anyone, it would have to be the person that handed him the drink from the sideline and maybe even the company that produced the drink.

What he didn't know was that it was all his mind at work. Once the central governor presented him with the red signals because he wasn't doing well, his mind began to lose faith in his abilities. The drink, however, didn't quite have an energy boosting component. It was just a placebo drink and once he gulped it, the placebo effect made him start trusting in the strength of the drink, therefore boosting his confidence. This goes to prove that most times, when your body starts telling you to stop, it is the brain that is safeguarding itself and, you have so much more to give. Although this theory is yet to be fully confirmed by scientists, it has been proven that something happens in the brain once you begin to expand an ample amount of energy. The drink, believed to be an energy booster, sent a signal to the brain, telling it that help has come. Thanks to this, it picks itself up, making you feel like your lost energy has been replenished. This means that most of the time, when your brain tells you that you can no longer go further because you are tired, you aren't tired. It is the almighty governor doing its job and with enough mindfulness, you can overcome this.

When you begin to gain control over your mind and thoughts, you begin to incredibly push the limits and do greater things than you could have ever imagined. In this case, your mind helps you realize what is really happening when your brain tells you that you can no longer go further. You will now realize that it is your brain that is craving some rest, but it doesn't mean you have reached your limit. Over time, you will be able to build your mental resilience when you understand the urge to quit and recognize it for what it is.

Don't Avoid Struggles, Seek Them Out

Most times, people tend to run away from struggles because they think that they are not strong enough to handle them. As you may already know, you are stronger than you think and if you are mindful enough, you can achieve much more than you have ever imagined. Aside from that fact that struggles help you gather experiences and knowledge, they also help you become stronger. Also, struggles help you become a better person and build your mental ability, so instead of trying to avoid them by laying on the couch watching TV, why not tap into the benefits that these struggles present and make the best out of them by facing them head-on. This will help you build your mental resilience. To do this, try to constantly push harder by testing your limits. Each time you do this, you will get a bit better. Of course, things will not get easier; they are bound to get more difficult as you proceed, but as you surmount each phase, you will grow and gather more mental and physical capacities to handle more difficulties. Let's say you are doing a squats routine. If you did fifty squats yesterday, today is the time to do ten more. Chances are that the previous day, once you reached forty squats, you thought you would collapse if you did even one more, but just a day later, you went all the way to fifty and are still standing. Today, forty will not feel that difficult anymore and later, you will go above fifty as you gradually get used to it.

When you become mindful, you realize that the thing you had so much fear for isn't that difficult after all. Soon, it becomes such a habit that you take up other challenges to keep you on your toes. It's all in your mind, so instead of seeking comfort, you can set out to push your limits.

When you set your mind to be tough and rugged, you will discover that there is almost nothing you can't do. Maybe the Biblical story of David and Goliath wasn't about divine power at work. It could have just been about a little man doing his absolute best because he knew everything in his existence depended on it. His brain may have seen a Goliath, but his mind saw a defeatable person, and indeed, he was able to triumph.

No matter what the physical tells you, all you need is to trust in the power of your mind. If your mind is set on achieving success, you will surely excel.

Chapter 2:
The Right Attitude is a Must

In life, you come across different people, go to different places, and experience different emotions. All these are what form your life experience. Now, have you ever wondered why two people may experience the same scenario differently? It is all about the state of your mind, which is simply your mindset. What may be difficult or scary to you may be fun and easy to someone else. The difference between you and the other person isn't farfetched. While you see a task as a challenge, the other person may see it as an adventure, and this is the reason why it will be a difficult task for you and not for the other person.

According to Charles R. Swindoll, life is 10% what happens to you and 90% how you perceive it. When faced with a challenge, however, it is up to you to choose whether to be reactive or proactive. When you allow your emotions to get the best of you and react according to the adrenaline rush in case of an emergency, chances are you will become overwhelmed by situations and lose control of everything. This means that when such things happen, you won't be able to handle them the way you should. It is a fact that there are times when emotions become so overwhelming that it may become impossible to not react to them, and when this happens, you must put your mind to work. If you become drawn to those emotions, it may be hard to get control of the situation. It may not even be something tied to emotion that seems to be overwhelming you, as it could be a certain procedure, an addiction, or just a phase. It is normal to get trapped in such situations. What makes you a strong person, however, is your ability to set your mind on your goal and evaluate the right and the not-so-right. In such situations, you have two choices; you can either be proactive or reactive.

If you are reactive, you will be highly affected by your environment. When things are good, you feel good, and when they aren't you feel terrible and almost always allow the tide of things to affect the way you perform and react. However, if you are proactive, you can set back and evaluate situations regardless of what effect they may have on you. The moment you feel down or when you seem to have been hit by a very hard blow, you have the power to catapult yourself to the point of absolute empowerment and strength.

In everything, consider being proactive, because in life, we are more inclined to choose the easy path as opposed to the difficult yet more profitable one. This may be a very difficult decision, but to become a proactive person, there are always steps to take. First, you must take responsibility for everything that happens, because this is what distinguishes you from a reactive person. As a proactive person, you

Relentless and Unbeatable

oversee your life and don't let external situations influence it. To do this, you must focus on things that are within your control. You see, there are some things that are absolutely beyond our control; such things will be the way they are no matter how much we brood over them. Instead of focusing your energy on such things, it is always better to look at the bright side and use the little or maybe not so little ray of light to your own advantage. Often, we can control the efforts, time and investment we put into certain things, but the results may not be entirely under our control. Therefore, when it comes to results, we must lay back to see what they turn out to be. This can be extremely difficult for some people, but the more we invest our time in things that we cannot control, the more time we lose neglecting the things that we can control, which may turn out to our advantage. Also, the problems may seem like much more than we can handle and the thought of them can be totally overwhelming. Instead of focusing on these problems, why not focus on the solutions? When you think about your problems too much, you create more problems by disarming yourself. Instead, you can gather strength by focusing your mind on the solutions. As soon as problems surface, think of how to solve them. In a way, these problems are part of the things you cannot control because they are already there. The part which you can control, however, is the possible way(s) to get rid of the problems. As a proactive person, you are already used to solving problems, so it's not a difficult thing to do at any point. You have discovered that the fastest way to get ahead in life is to act by finding a solution to your problem. Remember, when you focus on your problems, this creates more problems.

Consistency is another key aspect of being productive. If, at any point, you find that you are becoming indecisive, understand that you have derailed from the path of proactivity. As a proactive person, you must lean towards habits that propel you to achieving your goals. When you are consistent, you make progress, even if it feels like you are taking tiny inconsequential steps. With time, those seemingly small steps will earn you great results.

Your Life Depends on Your Mindset

In life, you have the power to change the way you see things, your perception of the people you come across, as well as your experiences. What you make of everything is largely up to you. Therefore, it is believed that you oversee your life. As discussed earlier, you can be a reactive person and leave your life to fate by letting everything slide, or you can be a proactive person and take absolute control of it. All this is a product of your mind and to excel, you need a positive mindset towards life.

The good thing is that we are in control of one of the most important tools in our existence, our mind. As each day passes by, we have the chance to make each minute meaningful by changing things to work in our favor. Sad day? Make yourself happy by looking at the good side of the bad experience. There is often so much to gain from one single thought, so take a deep breath and listen to your mind. A life-changing idea may just be about to pop in.

As a kid, there was a fairytale about a farmer who lived in a farmhouse that taught me how to see the good side of situations. One day, his only horse left home and did not return at night. His neighbors gathered to share their sympathy, and in such an unfortunate situation, they said, "how can this happen to you?" This farmer, almost unbroken, had only one thing to say: "Life goes on". The day after, his horse returned with a wild horse and having gone out to see if the new horse belonged to anyone, he discovered that he might just have to expand his barn to accommodate two horses. His good neighbors all gathered again, but this time to jubilate with him. Again, the farmer said, "Life goes on". The third day, the farmer's son went out with the wild horse, and while riding, he had an accident and broke his leg, and of course, the neighbors gathered and again, the farmer said, "Life goes on". A day after, Nazi soldiers went from house to house to recruit young men to join the army. When they got to the farmer's house, they rejected his son because he had a bad leg. Therefore, thanks to this farmer, I learned not to dwell on my problems. Though this is just a fairytale, the farmer did not dwell on his problems too much, even though it seemed like there was a new one every day. This is how we should lead our lives; instead of going on and on about the things that have gone wrong, the farmer chose to focus on the future.

Unlike the farmer though, we are advised to find permanent solutions while keeping our eyes on the future.

Although you must look at the bright side, it is important to be realistic. Remember that your life is not a fairytale, so you must take absolute charge of it. Try to be as forgiving as possible, and make sure you take a lesson from everything and everyone you come across. Somewhere, somehow, something great lurks around the corner, waiting to be found. Make sure you are determined to find it. Knowledge is power, so make sure your arm yourself with it by constantly searching for it. The fact that you do not know something does not mean that it does not exist. It also does not mean that it exists either, but if you don't attempt to find it, you will continue to live in oblivion, so step out of your comfort zone to enrich your mind. This single piece of information may be what you need to make a life-changing decision.

There are mistakes that are okay to make, as you can always learn from them. However, it is terrible to beat yourself up about them. Remember, they are in the past, and your past is one of the things you cannot change, so never focus on your mistakes and rather move ahead and implement the lessons you have learned from them. Do not think anyone is looking at the things you have done wrong, because in reality no one really cares, and you are the only one focusing so much on those mistakes. Life goes on, so move along with it so that you are not left behind because things are going to keep happening, with or without you.

Taking a moment to look within yourself works like magic. Pause and reevaluate your existence. Just sit with yourself and exist. Remind yourself of the things you stand for and the things that make you who you are. Look at the things you want from life, create dreams, and chase them. There are things that will exist between you and those dreams, and it is now up to you to either consider them obstacles that can hold you back, or forms of encouragement that will propel you to achieve greater things. Everything borders on your mindset and the way you interpret obstacles has to do with your perception and interpretation, which are core components of your existence. Remember we talked about consistency? Now, try to look at the mirror and look at yourself from someone else's point of view. Can you recognize the person in the mirror? If the answer is yes, it means that you have been consistent enough. If you said no, it means that somewhere along the line, you have deviated from the person you used to be. Maybe you need to retrace your steps, or perhaps change is what you need to get to the place you need to be. You don't have to be rigid; change when you should but do not be unnecessarily wavered. If you find out that you are beginning to lose control, maybe it is time to get your life back and take charge of it. Always remember that what lays in your mind has the full power to make or spoil your life. It all depends on you.

Chapter 3:
A Navy SEAL'S Mindset

Navy SEALs are known to be the most well-trained special force in the US Military and are even regarded by some as the most well-trained special force in the world. From BUDS training, Hell Week, and every other activity in the quest to become a Navy SEAL, it is not a weak mind's job to successfully complete the Navy SEAL training. Many people believe that being a Navy SEAL has everything to do with a person's physical structure, but this is not true because most times, the physique of a person doesn't go a long way to determine the success of a person in Navy SEAL training. You are probably wondering what determines the success of a Navy SEAL. Is it luck, genetics or fate, one may ask? Well, the reality is that the success of the Navy SEAL is not determined by the body, but by the mind.

According to experts, the SEAL training is specially designed to push you to the edge repeatedly until you either break or become tough and able to take up any task with confidence.

Don't Procrastinate

Relentless and Unbeatable

Procrastination is a killer of dreams. Whenever you think of an idea and you do not act when you are supposed to, those dreams are as good as dead. Procrastination makes you think you still have time, but the truth is, if you are not using it properly, time will never be enough. There is absolutely no difference between you and the multimillionaire that keeps cashing out despite bad government policies and even sometimes recession. You and the man that never cries about hard times have the strongest tool to succeed ever - time. Every single person has the same 24 hours to make a difference. Once you step out of your bed, make sure you achieve the things that you have thought of in your mind. The conditions may not be right, such as facing bad weather, or if your car has just broken down, but those are only physical limitations, and you have the power to rise above the odds. Never say tomorrow as tomorrow never ends. Take that step today because now is the perfect time. It is important to do what is right, but it is even more important to do what is right when it's right. When you push activities aside, you may be setting yourself up for undue pressure. When you eventually decide to do the things that you have postponed for so long, you may be faced with limited time or worse still, you may not be able to meet the deadlines at all because so much time has passed with you telling yourself that you will do what you were supposed to do some other time. It may be the pressure of having to deal with so many activities that is weighing you down. Think of the SEAL whose life in BUDS training is always all about overcoming different trials yet must set goals for himself in order to get to the finish line. Procrastination is never a thing for a Navy SEAL; in fact, a SEAL is incomplete without challenges and what makes him successful is his ability to attack those challenges head-on. No matter how difficult it may seem, a Navy SEAL is trained to overcome difficult/life-threatening challenges. This should be the mindset of anyone that wants to get anywhere close to success. Attack any task as it comes, and never leave it to later, because if you can do it later, you can do it now as well. Always keep a notepad at hand, and whenever you think that you may have thought of a brilliant idea, jot it down. This is because spontaneous ideas can slip through your fingers with the speed of a jellyfish so do not wait; write it down and act on it as fast as possible.

Discipline Is Not Punishment, Embrace Your New Habits

There are times when you must face consequences for your reaction to things you have done or have failed to do. Other times, you just must step out of your comfort zone to put yourself in a better place to achieve the things you want. Whenever you are faced with such scenarios, keep in mind that you are going through a disciplinary phase and can only get better at it. A Navy SEAL goes through more than a thousand experiences where they must sacrifice their comfort for a greater goal. During Hell Week, a BUDS candidate is said to be allowed only four hours of sleep during the whole week. Worse still, during the training, their resilience is tested on so many fronts, which is why the Navy SEAL isn't about physical fitness, but more about mental fitness. Sometimes, when a BUDS candidate is underwater with SCUBA gear, an instructor creeps in to yank the oxygen mask off from him. That's not all; the instructor then ties the candidate's oxygen line in a knot. A feeble-minded candidate will only see this as a punishment and even a death sentence, so instead of letting himself die, he would rather give up and leave the training camp. Others who are successful at the training will see this as just another challenge and will find a way to get their gear to work again in order to breathe. This will happen repeatedly. However, the product of this exercise is to help the candidate attain the highest possible level of discipline, amongst other things. In the future, while facing life-threatening situations, instead of panicking, the candidate will look for the root cause of the situation to get themselves back in shape. In the face of such difficulty, instead of seeing it as an attack on your person, or as a punishment for your past failures, the SEAL learns that it is just another phase of their training and they only have one choice, which is to succeed. Those who will become successful will not see a disciplinary action as a punishment, but as sacrifices needed to be made to become better.

When you lose sleep over a project you are currently undertaking, you must see it as a necessity and a step to make you stronger and better. Do not beat yourself up for taking up such a humongous task that is taking so much from you. Always keep in mind that you are stronger than the task. As stated in the earlier sections of this book, there is a lesson to learn from every single experience or person you meet. In the same light, pay keen attention to the details and the tiny bits of lessons you learn from any disciplinary phase you encounter. In the future, this will help you tackle similar situations. These lessons may be immaterial, but they will certainly come in handy. Just like a Navy SEAL whose scuba gear has been yanked off, instead of simply relying on your impulse, you have made it a habit to calm your nerves. Make sure you carry this habit with you and apply it in other scenarios when your nerves seem to be raging.

The 10-Second Rule

Sometimes, things get so intense that the only thing you can be at that moment is confused. At such times, if someone asks you to describe your state of mind, you may only have one word; confused. Well, this is normal; even the best sometimes gets confused too, but it shouldn't last for too long. When one gets to that point, several impulses begin to pop up and you may even be tempted to act on these impulses. Well, taking impulsive decisions is as dangerous as not making a move at all. If you make a wrong move based on your impulse, everything you have built over time can come crashing down. Psychologists say most impulsive decisions are most likely irrational. Let's say you are driving by the corner and a cyclist has just crashed into you. Your impulse will automatically give you signals to rush out of the car and rage at the fact that the cyclist may have just destroyed your bumper. If you act on that impulse, there is a possibility to lose more than just your bumper: perhaps your phone was on your lap at the time of the crash and as you were rushing out, you dropped it and stepped on it, therefore causing more damage by crushing your phone's screen. In these types of situations, the 10-second rule comes in handy. So, in this scenario, once you notice that you have been crashed into, the best thing to do is to take a few seconds (ten seconds is recommended) to take a deep breath and recollect yourself. Within these seconds, you have the chance to recollect yourself and make a more rational decision. Now, you will have the chance to pull yourself together and save yourself the agony of losing even more due to the incident.

Let's revisit the SEAL whose SCUBA gear has been yanked off; if when he notices that his gear is off, he acts on impulse, he might panic, and this may lead to him drowning. SEALS, however, are experts in calming their nerves, so they will not be so impulsive. They therefore typically apply the 10-second rule, so they take ten seconds to recollect themselves before making any move. This helps to save a lot of things and in the end, you will be grateful for those short ten seconds you have taken. On its own, ten seconds may be a bit inconsequential, but its value is priceless, so the next time you are on the edge, instead of trusting your impulse which isn't reliable, take a moment to apply the 10-second rule.

Do Things Others Won't do

Most times, going with the crowd makes you fit in, but you do not want to just be another person in the crowd, as it is better to stand out than to fit in. Being the only one doing things differently may seem weird but in the end, it will certainly pay off. Here's the catch: when you must do the same thing as many other people, think of a unique way to go about it. It doesn't mean you are doing it wrong; there are a thousand and one ways to do things, so don't stick to the common one. These common ways may be stereotypical. It is left for you to find the other narrative and stick to it, and in the end, you will be a bit above the rest.

This will be a bit daring but it will help a lot. When every other person seems to be going the same way, this must mean that it's the easy way, and it may possibly lead to getting 60 percent of the desired result, which is just a little bit above average. Well, it's a passing mark, right? You are way better than that and if you set your mind towards it, you can do much better. Try doing it differently; don't go in the same direction as 99 percent of the others. Look at the other possible but not so easy options and choose the one that best suits your purpose. If you find the drive and pursue it, you will be able to achieve more than the others.

Think Long Term
There is a goal for every activity that you indulge in. Sometimes, the immediate goal may not really be worth it. Well, you need to

Relentless and Unbeatable

remember that what you are doing is not for immediate gains. Think beyond tomorrow and think long-term.

The Navy SEALs are said to always be setting goals for themselves. When facing a hard time, like the SEAL, think of the things you wish to achieve in the future. Before enrolling for a special force in the US Army, passion is an important driving force so when they go through all the rigorous tasks, they keep setting their sights on the bigger picture, which is the main reason why they enrolled in the first place. When they are underwater, they keep telling themselves that they cannot quit, because, first, they do not want to die, and second, they remind themselves that while quitting will give them temporary relief, they will later regret the fact that they didn't carry on because quitting means giving up on their dreams.

The 3-3-3 rule is very potent in this aspect. When you are taking a decision, think about the effect it will have in the next three months. Let's say you didn't plan for a child but just discovered that you are pregnant; you now have two choices, to get rid of the pregnancy or to have the baby. Before you decide what to do, think of the effect it will have on you in the nearest and distant future. Are you going to abort the baby? Well, this may give you the chance to pursue everything you wish to achieve and may make you feel good for a short while, but what happens in the next three years? If you are going to decide to start having babies then, what happens if you are unable to conceive? Then, in the next three decades, if you are still not able to conceive, how will you feel? Maybe things will not turn out this way, and you may be able to conceive at the time you plan to in the future, and the only thing you will have to deal with is your conscience. If this doesn't really feel like a consequence you are willing to face in the future, maybe you should try the next option, especially when it's not like you never wanted to have babies at all. Now, the other option is to keep the baby, right? Think of the phases of pregnancy; in three months, you will be in your first trimester, which is the most difficult phase of your pregnancy journey. How are you going to deal with the morning sicknesses, the hormonal imbalance, and so many other changes in your metabolism? In three years, remember that you must deal with some physical changes. You will now have to be responsible for someone else - are you going to live up to the task? What about the next three decades? What or who will that child be? At that time, will all the trouble be worth it? Does it look like a long-term goal you are willing to achieve? Now, weigh your options and choose the one that is best for you.

Life Isn't A Competition

When you are striving to be a better person than you were yesterday, focus on yourself because you are all that matters. Do not wage yourself against somebody else because you want to compete with them, as they are also running their own race, and everyone will get to where they are meant to be time. When you focus too much on someone else, you lose focus on your own self and this doesn't help your journey in any way.

In anything that you do, strive to be better by constantly improving with all the resources and time at your disposal. Being better than the person you were yesterday is a goal that you must achieve. In fact, the only person you should want to be better than is your old self. Keep improving by the day; no amount of improvement can be enough, but don't ever think of wanting to be better than someone else. Of course, it is good to be better than someone else, but don't make it a goal. Being better than someone else comes naturally, so don't force it. Keep working hard to improve, don't stop, and remember - the sky is wide enough for every bird to fly.

Chapter 4:
Simple Yet Effective Strategies to Strengthen the Mind

The mind is the kernel of everything that has to do with every individual, from a single idea to the huge milestones accomplished. It all starts from the mind and the healthier your mind is, the faster it becomes, and it becomes capable of things that would ordinarily seem impossible. Therefore, people are often advised to take their mental health seriously. It is never a good thing to have a mind that is void of ideas, so when people perform below expectations, we hear stuff like: "you must be out of your mind". In order not to be out of one's mind, one needs to strive to always feed the mind to become healthier and stronger. Daily activities can alter your state of the mind, especially when you live in a city that seems to have so many crazy things. In such cases, a person is faced with the battle of trying to keep a sane mind. On your own, this may be very difficult as so many factors contribute to keeping your mind healthy. Therefore, one must make conscious efforts to keep their mind healthy. The following are some tips to do so:

Relentless and Unbeatable

Wake up early and get out of bed: Sleep is a good thing and it would be detrimental to your health to not get enough of it. Just like everything that has a good side, it is wrong to spend most of your time sleeping. This will not only make you come across as a lazy person, but it also puts your mind in a state of idleness. Nothing productive ever comes out of an idle mind. Everyone is advised to get at least six hours of sleep. This means that if you go to bed by 10 PM, you shouldn't be up before 4 AM.

However, there is a huge difference between waking up and getting out of bed. Some people can take up to three hours to get up from their bed after waking up. While this habit gives one time to accommodate as many thoughts as possible, it also gives him time to leave so many things undone. So, this means that after getting enough sleep, a person is expected to wake up and get out of bed early. It is a known fact that every fresh morning offers enough energy to do much more than you will in the afternoon or at night, except in case of sickness. Once your mind, body, and brain have rested enough at night, your mind is re-energized, and you can do much more in the morning. The thing is that during your daily activities, you have very little control over how the day will turn out. That's why it's important for you to get up early to program your mind to work the way you want it to be so that you can set the tone for the rest of the day.

Make your bed: Once you get out of bed, don't just walk away. Take a few seconds to look back at the mess you made while sleeping. Do you want to leave that mess behind? I guess you wouldn't like to start your day on that note, so take some time to make your bad. This has both a physical and mental effect on you. The time you use to make your bed gives you the chance to think. You will be able to think of the things you want to achieve that day. Also, you will be able to articulate yourself and get yourself together before even stepping in the shower. On the other hand, this simple exercise will boost your mental strength. Looking at your neatly made bed will automatically make you feel tidy and this is necessary to set the tone for the day. As you have already started the day on that note, you will possibly want every part of your day to be like that, starting from the remaining parts of your room. Oh! That shirt isn't in its right place, so put it where it needs to be, and the same goes for every other thing and like magic, you will find out that you ran through the remaining part of your day calm and collected.

Carry heavy shit: Your physical and mental wellbeing works together, and therefore it is important to be as physically as mentally fit. Every day make sure you test your strength by trying to lift something heavy. This will help you flex your muscles as well as remind you that you have so much energy lurking within you. You may not have the time to go to the gym or the willpower to take on an exercise routine. Lifting something heavy once or twice will help you make up for the little exercise you are missing out on.

Relentless and Unbeatable

Study first: There is nothing more important than reading books. Every book has a unique idea to offer, so always make sure you pick up a book and look out for that singular idea that will work for you, no matter how little it may seem. Reading can create new ideas within you and light up your imagination. This is because the ideas imbibed in a book do not exist in isolation. As you are digesting it, it interacts with some of the knowledge that you already have and the idea you can gain from each book, no matter how small, will add more flavor to the state of your mind.

Eat something you don't like: The importance of eating healthy can never be overemphasized. Food is an integral requirement of your everyday life. So, it is important to eat good food, even if you do not like its taste. For example, kids are known to hate vegetables even though they are very good for their health. The fact that they do not like them doesn't mean that parents won't give it to them. Typically, parents and food companies find ways of infusing it into children's diets without them realizing it. You can employ the same strategy. Maybe you hate carrots, but you need Vitamin A for better sight; so, instead of avoiding it, you can simply blend it into your food and make it a way of adding color to it. This goes for every other food you do not like. Remember that a healthy diet is the cradle of good health, so make sure you eat well. You do not have to like the food; just eat what is right because it is important for your health.

Chapter 5:
From Fragile to a Champions Mind

In this chapter, I am going to show you how to transform your mind from the unconscious programming that has led you to believe that you have been stripped of your innate ability to be a winner. If you follow the strategies outlined here (and in other chapters of this book), you will feel like screaming from the rooftop "bring it on, world, bring it on!"

You Are Your Own Leader

From birth and all through your childhood, you have been accustomed to look up to others (parents, guardians, influential persons) for direction and leadership. They told you what to do, how to do it, and when to do it, and you accepted it all; line, hook, and sinker. Well, that was in your formative years. As an adolescent, your instinct to rebel against ideas that do not resonate with you began to surface, but if you are like most people, those instincts were quickly squelched by the people you looked up to. They prefer to keep you under control; that way, they can lead you to the "right path."

Relentless and Unbeatable

Docile and broken, a lot of people allowed that type of programming to govern their lives even into adulthood, and it reflects in every facet of their lives. They look up to governments to make their economy better, look up to their bosses to make their working conditions better or to give them directions, and look up to their partners (spouses, business associates, etc.) to tell them if what they are doing is in order or not. At best, most people only offer suggestions and hope that those suggestions have a favorable response.

Athletes are not immune to this type of programming or upbringing, so it is not surprising to find athletes with very strong minds. Just observe an athlete (or any individual for that matter) and see how they make up their minds about a course of action, and you can tell if they are operating from a fragile or an unbeatable mindset. But the good news is, even if you are operating from the subconscious programming of a fragile mind, you can turn that around. And here's exactly how to do that.

- Recognize that you are an individual with a complete mind of your own.

- Accept that you have the sole responsibility for the outcomes of your decision.

- Challenge your mind to come up with decisions and answers without waiting for someone else.

- Pay attention to suggestions from external sources but allow your mind to decide if those suggestions are fit for you or not.

- Do not be afraid to make decisions.

- Do not be afraid to make the wrong decisions.

- Give yourself permission to voice your views.

I am not in any way suggesting disregarding constituted authority. I am only stating the obvious: you do not have to rely on anyone to know what to do and how to do it. The truth is, every possible method that has been proposed to perform an action was from someone's mind – a mind that took charge and was not afraid to be put to test. Such minds are in no way better than yours! You are well-equipped and capable of looking inwards to determine what suits you best and to come up with decisions based on your deep convictions. If you really want to succeed and stand out from the crowd, don't wait for directions. You must carve out a path and tread it without caring if anyone is following or not. Remember, others have the inalienable right to direct their own lives too.

It takes practice, but when you begin to give your mind the permission to come up with its own ideas, it is like exercising a muscle; with time, it will develop, and soon, you can make split-second decisions that are very sound and have positive outcomes.

You are the boss of your life. Always remember that! It is time to take back the wheels of control and flush out the feebleness and flawed programming drummed into you during your formative years. Authority figures are good, but you must understand that you are an authority of your own!

There's Always Room for Improvement

What's your highest achievement? Really, what is it? Write it down. Now, below that, write in bold letters, "I CAN DO BETTER THAN THIS!" (And make sure to include the exclamation mark). Please, when doing this exercise, do not type the words using your computer, phone, tablet, or any other device. Use a pen and paper, as there is a flow of energy that occurs when you write words with your hands from your mind onto a paper. It is like birthing an idea from the realm of the unseen (the mind) into physical reality (paper). That is the very first step to creating from your mind.

You see, no matter your level of achievement, your mind can think of several other ways to do better than your previous achievement. Remember Napoleon Hill's famous quote? "*Whatever the mind of man can conceive and believe, it can achieve.*" Now, that's not just some fine saying; it is a fact. There is no limit whatsoever that exists in your mind except what you have accepted as your limits. We have spoken about this in Chapter 1, as we mentioned that there are physical limits but none whatsoever for the mind (kindly go back to Chapter 1 if you skipped it).

I'll let you in on a little secret that can change your entire life and career. Most of us are guilty of settling for a standard we accept instead of striving for the success we have imagined for ourselves. You can surpass whatever you have accomplished in the past unless you have decided to settle for your past achievement as your peak accomplishment. In that case, you have accepted a standard instead of continuing to strive to greater heights.

Realize that once you have accomplished a task or reached a milestone in your life or your career, that accomplishment is in the past. Basking in it is simply living in the past! While there is nothing wrong with enjoying the good feeling that comes with reaching your goals, dwelling on it is the same as telling your mind that you have reached your destination, so it can take a break and circle back to that point whenever the need arises. This makes it impossible for you to go beyond that success level. Do you see how a feeble mind can keep you stuck perpetually? And if you find yourself in a situation where you seem not to be able to surpass your previous achievements, it is time to break free from the vicious circle. Here's how.

- Do the exercise above, i.e., write down your highest achievement and in bold letters write "I CAN DO BETTER THAN THIS!"

- In your mind's eye, visualize yourself breaking your own records, no matter how laudable they are.

- Challenge your mind to think of ways to improve on your previous accomplishments.

Remember your past actions that brought about those accomplishments and begin to take greater and more intelligent actions that are sure to produce greater results (read the section *Start Counting When You're Tired*).

More Than One Way

There is no beeline to success, so quit looking for it. You will make mistakes! That's a given. When you understand and accept this fact, you will save yourself the heartache of wallowing in self-pity because your attempt at success didn't yield the result you wanted. However, if you acknowledge that mistakes or temporal setbacks are what make you do something better the next time, there is no room to categorize your mistakes as a failure. When others see that you have failed, this creates a clear pathway to improving by doing the same thing in a better way.

A feeble mind easily accepts failure. An unbeatable mind does not recognize the word "failure" – it simply forges ahead despite failure. Come to think of it - why should you accept failure when there is obviously more than one way to do something? Do you see why it is important to give your mind permission to think for itself? If you do, your mind is intelligent enough to come up with dozens of ways for you to do one thing. So, if one way does not yield the expected result, don't just shut down your mind, throw your hands in the air in exasperation and cry "I know I'm not cut out for this stuff!" Yes, you are, but only if you will allow your mind to show you other ways to do the same thing.

Look intelligently at your past failures and you will see that because you improved on them, you were able to succeed at things that seemed impossible before. I love using the example of the latest automobiles. For example, look at the design of the 1964 Mercedes Benz 220 series. Considering that in retrospect, it is a complete failure compared to the performance of the latest series. However, designers and engineers kept on improving on past failures until the present 2019 Mercedes Benz CLS series. And if you think that is an awesome model, wait until 2050 and you may consider the latest model a complete failure too.

But I am not just referring to cars. I am asking you to look at your very first achievement in your field and see how far you've come. If you've been in your field for around 5 years, you will notice that your early achievements would be considered gross underperformance if you were to repeat those "feats" now. In other words, your mind constantly strives to outperform its previous achievements, but only if you allow it.

So, stop seeing failure as the end of the road. It is only a pathway to create numerous other paths for you to explore. If you approach your endeavors with this mindset, nothing can stop you from attaining your goals.

Pressure Brings Out the Best in You

10 months ago, your maximum pushup count was 100. Today, it is still 100. Does that not tell you there is something fundamentally wrong with your mind? Your mind cannot go beyond 100 pushups; therefore, your body cannot surpass that number. In fact, you have found a comfort zone and you are unwilling to leave it. There is no pressure, so it feels like home. I've got news for you. When it begins to feel like home, your best is gradually dying away!

When you are no longer under pressure, your mind is no longer attentive – its heightened sensitivity is dulled by a lack of challenge. It begins to lose its ability to function optimally. Here's a quick example: when do you feel more alive and active to do your daily activities; is it when you are a bit hungry or when you are full and satiated? Obviously, when you are a bit hungry, you find the physical vigor and mental alertness to perform your activities well. (Have you considered why many people find it more fulfilling to exercise on empty stomachs, especially in the mornings?) But when you have eaten and are full, your cognitive functions become a bit dull. Your brain simply lulls you to relax or even take a nap. Why? It has reached its climax – there is no more pressure to seek satisfaction, so the next natural thing to do is simply to relax.

In the same vein, when your mind senses that there is no longer any pressure, it dulls you and your best does not come to fore. That is why if you want to grow your mind to the point of being unbeatable, you must welcome pressure. You should cherish the moments when there is pressure because those are the times you come out shining. For those who do not wish to leave their comfort zone, pressure puts them in an uncontrollable situation, but for you, it is a welcomed development and you are more than able to control such situations.

An unbeatable mind:

- Does not panic in the face of pressure; it is always calm, cool, and collected.

- Sees pressure as a stepping stone.

- Shines brighter in the face of adversity.

- Knows the importance of constant growth; therefore, it seeks opportunities to step out of its comfort zone.

Start Counting When You're Tired

Picture an athlete doing 100 pushups and counting from the first pushup. At the hundredth, they are done and move on to something else. Well, that's one way to do 100 pushups. Here's another way: do as many as you can until you are tired, then begin to count from 1. If you can get to 100, you have truly accomplished something worth celebrating. (And I am not just referring to pushups alone). This is a simple tactic to break a previous record. Take yourself to the height where you have been before, then begin to convince your mind that that level is your starting point! This will keep you going when most other people would have quit. It doesn't matter in what area of life you apply this technique - it works all the time.

It is the unconscious programming that kicks in to tell you that you cannot go beyond a certain point. It is your fragile mind that puts up the imaginary barrier and cajoles you into thinking that it is real. And as a matter of fact, your mind can easily come up with concrete evidence to show you how impossible it is to hit your target. And if you are like most people, you will cower in obeisance and accept that limitation.

But if you are tired of being told what you can or cannot do (whether by your fragile mind or from external sources), you will most definitely:

Be the first person in and certainly the last person out.
Continue working and giving it, one more tries even when others have given up or said it can't be done.

Be the one with an incredible work ethic.

There's something liberating when you understand the power of your mind. As much as it shapes your world, it can only do so from the information you feed it. So, if you constantly feed your mind with debilitating thoughts such as, "I can't go any further", "it's just impossible", "no one has been able to do this", etc., your intelligent mind will dutifully surround you with evidence to prove you right. On the flip side, if you honestly think and feel, "it's not over until I succeed", "I know I can do this", "I am built for this", guess what? Those thoughts fuel your mind to create a reality that matches them.

However, you should realize that it takes a considerable amount of time for your mind to be transformed from a fragile state into an unbeatable state, just as it took a long time for your authority figures to (unintentionally) drum mediocrity into you.

Stay Humble... No Matter What!
Did you read the part where I said not to disregard constituted authority? Well, I meant it. If not checked, the feeling of success has a way of making people cocky. And you know what they say - pride comes before a fall.

As much as I want you to have an unbeatable mind (which, by the way, is not negotiable if you want to succeed), you must also develop an attitude to put pride in its rightful place. However, aside from success making people proud, tough situations also have a way of making people rebel against constituted authority.

Your trainer, for example, may put you through rigorous training that will bring you to your breaking point (we all have them). And at that point, you may feel like giving up and walking away. But if you recognize that discipline is not punishment (as discussed earlier in Chapter 2) and accept that your success is the goal, you will most likely embrace the process and humbly learn to develop the habits that are being instilled in you.

Here are a few ways to help you keep your head down no matter what:

- Keep your focus on the result even if the process is unpleasant.

- Pain is temporary; the gain is worth it.

- Get your mind off the pain and your body will feel it less; mind over matter works every time.

- If you are training with others, consider the possibility that you are an inspiration to both your colleagues and your trainer.

- You are growing into an authority in your field, so stay humble so that others are humble towards you too.

As I bring this chapter to a close, let me quickly elaborate on an important point I mentioned in an earlier paragraph. We all have breaking points; I mean, that's why we are humans, right? This book is aimed at making you tough mentally, but I do not intend in any way to make you toughen up to the point of being suicidal. There are some physical strains that are not suitable for everyone. Recognizing your physical limits and drawing the line at that point will enable you to stay physically safe to accomplish whatever it is you desire. Going beyond your physical limitation is not advised as it may jeopardize your physical health and by extension, your mental health too. Therefore, I strongly urge you to know your physical limits and make your activities fit into your known boundaries. This is not to say you cannot be, do, or have whatever your mind conceives and believes. Always remember this: even though there are physical limits, there are none for the mind!

Chapter 6:
The Hidden Rule to Push Yourself to the Limit

Ever wondered how Navy SEALs are so mentally tough?

And no, they are not superhumans. They are humans like you who have mastered the art of breaking their mental barrier and overcoming their limitations. Thanks to this, they can rise above the boundaries of their flesh and complete any task successfully.

The SEALs believe that no matter how tired you feel, you are still far from your limit and you are still capable of so much more. In short, the feeling of fatigue is the brain's way of shying away from pain.

"It's a way of saying that by drawing on our mental strength we can push through any situation. When the chips are down, tell yourself you have at least 40 percent left in the tank." (Jesse Itzler)

The 40% Rule: Any Scientific Backing?

If you look at the 40% rule critically, you will notice that it is not a rule. Instead, it's another way of saying you are capable of so much more than you think. Hence, when you feel like you have reached your limit, you are a few miles away from your starting point.

Hence, whether we call it the 20%, 30% or 45% rule doesn't matter. What matters is the fact that your mind should be the one to determine how far you go, and not your muscles.

There is a lot of research to support the fact that it is your brain, not your muscles that determines your endurance strength and limit. We have been made to believe that muscles get tired because we physically can't go on any longer. Hence, we are unable to continue our task because we exhausted fuel or the buildup of metabolites – the byproduct of muscle contraction.

> *Professor Tim Noakes in 1990 revealed that the brain limits your muscle to prevent it from going to exhaustion. (Christian Finn)*

In a bid to prevent exhaustion, the brain triggers the distressing signals that it is time to quit. This is when you feel muscle fatigue.

This is your brain restricting you from tapping into your reserve in a bid to make you have the provision in case of an emergency.

The 40% Rule: Key to Unlocking Your Mental Toughness

There is something that separates high performers from ordinary people. High fliers and people we think as superhuman are ordinary people that have learned to overcome the mental barrier many are faced with.

In understanding the 40% rule, it is essential to explain why our brain sometimes holds us back.

Civilization at Breakneck Speed

From the beginning of times, humans have been known to fight to survive, and this has conditioned the brain to do everything it can to keep us alive. In the past, humans mainly fought this way to meet basic living needs, as well as to fight threats, infections, and disease. Our forefathers had a lot of things against them.

However, as the years passed, development began, which translated into a developed quality of life. Our health system makes use of sophisticated technology, and man is not limited in transportation as airplanes can take you just about anywhere.

Many people have access to a quality life, fresh food, and shelter, and this development came at a mighty speed.

The Human's Primitive Brain

This development was quick and beneficial to man. However, our brain could not keep up with the pace. While humans have evolved into the twentieth century, the brain is still in primitive days. So many things our forefathers usually struggled with are now readily available.

Ultimately, this means that humans have more time to worry about other things. Humans now crave to enjoy life, as well as to be recognized and feel fulfilled. Even with this development, we still react instinctively to our environment.

Even if hardly facing any danger, the brain exaggerates the slightest bit of it. This was very useful to our forefathers as it ensured their survival. However, life and society have evolved, but the brain couldn't keep up with this way of life.

Since the brain is lagging in this regard, it is more after our comfort and wellbeing. It prioritizes comfort and dreads every sign of harm or stress. The brain has been programmed to restrict and flee at the slightest tendency of risk and danger all in a bid to keep us alive.

This has made man limited, which manifests itself when we run a marathon but stop halfway because we feel like we can't go on. You can also feel this when trying intermittent fasting in a bid to lose weight, but every fiber of your being keeps screaming that you are going die. You give up on everything you set your heart to, even though you already overcame the reluctance of starting.

In a bid to keep us alive, our brain encourages us to give up for short-term comfort.

The 40% Rule
It is impossible to completely overcome the resistance from our brain when we set out to start a task that seems confusing. But the good news is that we can gradually rise against it, nipping it in the bud with

Relentless and Unbeatable

every hard task we undergo. So, you can train your brain to recognize and get over the mental barrier that keeps you stagnant.

The 40% rule is quite simple. When you think you are done, when you feel you have used up all your capacity, when you feel like you lack the will and mental strength to keep going – you have just exhausted 40% of your ability. In other words, when many people get to the point of quitting, only 40% of their physical and mental strength has been exhausted. Many people are full of great things and capable of so much more. Hence, when you realize that you still have so much left in your tank, it does seem horrible to throw in the towel, doesn't it?

The 40% principle was the effort of Jesse Itzler, a Californian billionaire entrepreneur in his life-changing book – 'Living with a Seal.' The 40% rule originates from a time when Jesse and a set of other people had a 24-hour race to complete. During this endurance race, Jesse met with David Goggin's, a US Navy SEAL who chose to run the entire marathon solo.

Despite all odds, David resisted the urge to quit and kept going. He was able to complete the race even with a broken bone, which fascinated Jesse. Inspired by his unique mental strength, Jesse wondered how he pulled through. In a quest to know his secret, he asked David to be his mentor. David agreed, on the condition that Jesse will do everything he is asked without exception.

After a month, David moved to go live with Jesse and the Itzler's. This led Jesse to discover things he never knew or believed he was capable of. With David as his mentor, he was able to do 100 pull-ups when he thought he was capable of just eight. David put him through many crazy things that led Jesse to conclude that everyone is capable of so much more.

Training the Brain

The fact many people need to understand is that when you feel like you have given it everything you've got, you haven't. Yes, this is difficult, but to develop your mental strength, you've got to ignore those pesky warning signals from your brain and subject yourself to discomfort. With time, you can learn and train yourself to push through any task set before you.

When you train your brain, you should have three things in mind. The effort to overcome the inertia, the firm determination to block out that little pesky voice asking you to quit and the patience to keep doing what you set out to do. Whenever you are on the verge of giving up, bear in mind that these are false signals from the brain to avoid stress. Be strong enough to resist it.

Bear in mind that the resistance will come. When it does, be mindful of it and take it as a clue that you are far from doing even half of what you are capable of.

Many of our limitations come from ourselves, and we are capable of way more than we think. One thing you have got to know about the 40% rule is that it must be in your subconscious. Walk with it, remember it whenever you are at the edge of giving up, and draw strength from it to push past your mental barrier. Also, this is just not about sports or physical activities. This applies to every area of our life – work, relationships, restrictions, etc.

Always remember, the human mind can either be your biggest asset or your largest undoing. The ball is in your court.

The 40% Rule: Developing Mental Toughness

The one secret to being resilient, to keep going despite all odds, and to persevere and give any task an extra push is to develop your mental toughness. This will keep you going, irrespective of things in life meant to dissuade you from your path/goal. While we acknowledge that developing mental toughness is not easy, it is possible. We will give you some tactics to build resilience in preparation for bullets and knocks life throws at you.

Before we dive into that, it is important to understand mental toughness.

What is Mental Toughness?

Mental toughness is the ability to persevere and keep going despite adversity and hardship. Mental toughness is what will allow you to keep your eyes on your goal despite all the difficulties you may be facing. Many times, we have high expectations and expect things to go how we want. When this doesn't happen, many people who lack mental toughness are quick to throw in the towel.

However, with mental toughness, you get to learn from your mistakes, so you can make a one and get back up without lamenting over the mess and the psychological devastation of failing. It is mental toughness that gives you the fuel and zeal to keep going when life throws stones at you and everything seems overwhelming.

You should see mental toughness as that tiny voice that motivates you against the will of your flesh. It is that personal encouragement that tells you to do just a little more and that encourages you to keep going when it gets tough and seems impossible.

Manage Your Expectations

To build resilience to the things that come your way, you have got to be careful of your expectations. When your expectations are not managed adequately, you may feel surprised and feel like everything is out of your control.

When they lack control, people tend to worry and become anxious. This ultimately affects your motivation, and this could affect your mental strength. By managing your expectations, you become flexible, ready, and able to adapt to any situation. This is the foundation for a healthy mental strength.

People with high mental strength have developed their ability to remain rigid and unchanged in the face of adversity. These are people that have learned to adapt when situations don't go as planned with the flexibility to seek other ways to tackle what is before them.

It is not about just rolling with the punches; instead, it is about devising ways to take a swing. It is high time you understand that many things will happen that will be out of your control. However, the one thing you can control is your reaction. Always look at situations from a different perspective. If your vision is already tinted with the shade of instant emotional response, you will not be able to objectively understand and see things in their true color. Rather, if you have the time, wait for a couple of minutes before responding. Many people instantly react to an issue without even fully understanding the matter. Be sure to understand any case before you, then put the pieces together.

The following are tricks to becoming flexible and managing your expectations.

Redefine Your Reality

The way to keep your expectation realistic is to understand them. While we have no control over surprises, a good idea to prepare ourselves is to anticipate the likely outcome of an issue. When you understand your expectations, you can be honest with yourself and form realistic ones. Therefore, it is a bad idea to rely on possibilities or to put so much faith in your expectations. This sets you up for disappointment when things don't go as planned.

The ability to anticipate and accept outcomes will make you healthy, prepared, and unmoved by surprises when they come.

Don't Let Emotions Get the Best of You
While it is an excellent idea to be in touch with your emotions, at times, they can also cloud your judgment. Most times, emotions do not allow people to approach situations objectively. Developing emotional resilience is critical in fighting through difficult conditions.

According to the 40% rule, it is emotions that make people give up quickly rather than keep going. A simple way to build and improve on your emotional resilience is to own whatever situation you find yourself in, rather than run towards comfort – and yes, this is the approach most people opt for, as it is the easy way out!

Taking the easy way out means never getting out of your comfort zone. This will rob you of vital lessons and of the benefits of perseverance. There is no way you can know how much you know until you try to know. However, if you don't try to know, if you don't give yourself the chance of proving that you can do it, there is no way you can know.

Form the habit of getting comfortable in stressful situations as this will help deal with stress. *According to the SEALs, you must get comfortable being uncomfortable.*

To keep going when things get tough is the boost you need to stay calm when things go haywire. While being in touch with your emotion is right, be sure to be in control.

Always Be in Touch with Your Motivation

Without the needed motivation, managing your expectations and taking charge of your emotions will not get you far. Whatever task you are faced with, you need inner motivation to keep going. To push through in the face of that difficult task, you need the motivation to keep going.

- To become motivated, you have got to ask yourself "why?"

- Why am I doing this?

- Why do I need to push through?

The answers to these questions are key to understanding why you should keep going. However, bear in mind that your answers shouldn't be "because I have to", because in the face of something challenging, you do not always have a choice.

Instead, set a specific goal and consider a third party or someone that depends on you. A person may be trying to lose weight to be more attractive, so they may give reasons like:

- Because I want to feel attractive

- Because I want to avoid diseases that come with obesity

- Because my family and friends need me alive

Knowing why it is important to see something through makes facing it easier. It doesn't stop here though, because you must break the barriers that come with this. This happens through strong willpower and mental strength. Building these up takes time but is possible.

When you accomplish a small task, you get to boost your willpower, leading to an improvement in confidence. This helps you realize how much you can do and how far you can go, ultimately helping you believe in yourself.

Willpower is said to be inexhaustible, and in fact, you have as much willpower as you think you have. With this, you have got to challenge yourself and access your motivation, and surmounting obstacles will be easier than you think.

Come to Terms with Delayed Gratification

Relentless and Unbeatable

One of the best success strategies is accepting things as they are and learning to accept failure. However, it doesn't come easy as it requires mental toughness.

Being mentally tough encompasses many things. One of them is the ability to delay gratification or to not jump at instant gratification. Always be mindful of the fact that nothing good comes easy. As a result, if you can persevere, work hard, and patiently wait, you will get the grasp of what mental toughness is about.

Mistakes will happen along the way, but do not dwell on them. Things might not go the way you want, but with time and patience, you can accomplish what you set your heart to.

Mental toughness requires denying yourself, telling yourself no, and developing the patience to stand by your decision.

You will be faced with a couple of things that are not worth your time. However, never let go of the mindset that whatever comes your way, you can see it all the way through.

It is important to note that mental toughness does not come overnight. You have got to be determined, patient and consciously strive towards rising against all odds. Equipping yourself to handle all the horrible blows life throws at you comes back to developing mental toughness. This happens via reasonable expectations, true motivation, and getting hold of your emotions.

Chapter 7:
How to Create Confidence when Humiliated

Many people are of the opinion that some people are born with confidence and that these few lucky people have this inherent gift and can walk into a room and take charge. People think that they naturally draw people towards them as a result of their charisma and self-confidence.

However, I must disprove that. Confidence is a skill and quality that comes with practice. In short, if you are the timid person ever, you can take actionable steps to build your self-confidence and lead people. With constant effort and practice, you can take steps to improve your confidence to lead.

Besides being a leader, self-confidence is a terrific quality that will set you apart. People are naturally drawn to confident people as they tend to have the charm and magic to command others. As crucial as self-confidence is, many people see it as a difficult task. However, a lack of confidence could make one terrible at being a leader, whatever field they're in.

This explains why people find it difficult to invest in an idea being aired by a fidgety, nervous, and timid dude. While on the other hand, someone who is knowledgeable, holds his head high, admits his ignorance, and answers your entire question brilliantly will not find it difficult to turn prospects into customers.

Confident people make others sure, and therefore it is an essential attribute for a leader. Besides, to be successful as a leader, you have got to be able to gain the confidence of other people.

Building confidence as a leader does not need to be a daunting task. With the right effort, you can build and learn faith, which is well worth the effort.

What Is Self-Confidence?

There are two significant factors that determine self-confidence: self-efficacy and self-esteem.

The process of mastering skills, setting goals and seeing them to completion, and achieving dreams in yourself and even in other people is a vital key to gaining self-efficacy. In other words, this confidence stems from the fact that focusing on developing and mastering a field or area will help you succeed. This is what gives people the motivation and challenge to accept and face a seemingly impossible task to the end, despite many setbacks.

Self-efficacy goes hand in hand with the idea of self-esteem. Self-esteem is the school of thought that we have control of things that happen in our life and can accept it. However, some of this is due to the assurance that people we know and love such as friends and families approve of us, which is usually out of our control. Also, part of it comes from the fact that we know we are skilled at what we do, are at our best, and can achieve whatever we set our heart to.

There are many things that you can do to gain the confidence to lead, from building your skills, to affirmation, to positive thinking. This is what this chapter seeks to explore. And, when you are done reading this chapter, I hope you understand that self-confidence and the confidence you need to be a leader is a skill you can learn. It is not a skill restricted to a group of people.

Building Self-Confidence to Lead

How do you develop your confidence to lead? How will you build the charisma that sets you out as an exceptional leader whom others are naturally drawn towards?

While there is no quick fix or secret formula, it is possible. With diligence, dedication, and determination, you can build self-confidence which will translate to success in everything you set your heart to. The best part is that the tips and tricks to building confidence automatically set you on the path to success. You should not forget that confidence comes from tangible achievements that stay with you for life.

To build the confidence to lead, we will focus on three metaphors and provide you with as many tips as possible.

Step1: Getting Set for The Journey

To develop the confidence to lead, you have got to be set for the journey. In other words, consider your starting point and your destination. It is not all about physical preparation alone, but mental preparation as well. You must do a lot of things to prepare yourself for the journey ahead.

The following are some steps to get set for the journey:

Don't Lose Sight of Your Achievements

In other words, create an achievement journal. And if you will be leading a team, allow stubborn projects you led your team to inspire you. Deals you were able to close and prospects you successfully turned to clients etc. are achievements that can keep you going as a leader. It can even be as simple as an idea that changed the course of your business.

When the going gets tough, get in the habit of coming back to these achievements and draw strength from them. Look at them every morning and let them inspire you to do better. The power that comes from knowing you are successful is enough to give you the needed zeal to keep pushing in the face of discouragement. By doing so, you gradually build your confidence.

Ensure to update this achievement log from time to time. Whenever you achieved a goal that you have set, proudly engrave it in gold on your record and add tougher ones.

Reflect on Your Strength

This technique is like a SWOT analysis to consider who you are and where you are headed. Still drawing inspiration from your achievement journal, try and analyze your strengths and weaknesses. To get honest opinions, asking your friends and family is an excellent idea.

Consider the Things That Matter

In your quest to build your confidence to lead, you have got to prioritize things that matter as well as your goals with the team. You have got to set achievable goals, in your interest as well as the interest of the people you are leading. This is one of the ways to truly gain confidence.

When you set goals, you establish your targets and judge your success based on reaching such targets. Also, allow your SWOT analysis to guide you. In other words, capitalize on your strengths, reduce your weaknesses, bank on your opportunities, and control your threats.

Take Control of Your Mind

This is where you have got to get your mind in order. Be sure to identify those pesky little voices in the back of your head that damage your self-confidence. Try and think positively.

Make it a habit to employ the power of positive mental imagery to create sharp images of how it will feel like to reach your goal. Imagine the satisfaction that comes from this. Draw strength from it as there is a sense of possibility that comes from this that makes even the hardest goal seem achievable.

Commit Yourself to Success

To develop your confidence to lead, the final piece of the first puzzle is to commit yourself to the goals you have set. In other words, promise yourself you can do it and that you will give it all it takes to complete what you set your heart to.

While this might lead to self-doubts, don't ignore them. Take note of them and rationally challenge them. Identify the reason for the uncertainty and devise strategies to counter them. If your doubts come from genuine concerns, ensure to come up with additional procedures to remove them.

Final Tips on Getting Set for The Journey

Developing the confidence to lead should always be about balance. There are two extremes; on one side, there are people that suffer from low confidence, while on other, some may come off as overconfident.

Being underconfident will limit you as you will hardly come out of your comfort zone and will not stretch yourself, robbing you of knowing what you are capable of. On the other hand, excessive confidence could come back and hurt you as well because you overstretch yourself and the team and bank on things beyond your capacity, making you crash.

You have got to get things right and make sure to balance your self-confidence. This should be based on your real strengths. Just the perfect amount of self-confidence to lead will help you take calculated risks, stretch yourself to achieve your limits, and not view tasks as insurmountable.

Step 2: Launch Out

This is where you start gradually, adding bricks on top of bricks to your wall of confidence, getting closer to your goal with every step you take. Every passing day, you focus on an essential task and enjoy the easy wins and small goals that add up to the big one. You are on the path to success, improving your confidence as you go on.

In launching out, the following are tips that gear you towards building your confidence:

Gather the Essential Knowledge and Experience

With your target in mind, you have got to identify the right skill you need to make it a reality. The confidence to be a leader comes from mastering the required expertise to lead your team towards reaching their goals.

We are not talking about sketchy skills just to get the job done. It is about acquiring the skill that adds to your wealth of knowledge and experience. This doesn't mean just coming up with a 'good-enough' solution. This is something that sets you out as knowledgeable. The feeling of being knowledgeable alone can give you the needed boost to lead effectively.

Don't Forget the Basics

Developing the confidence needed to lead is not about trying something clever or trying to impress. It is not about being perfect either, as confident people own up to their mistakes. Hence, in your journey towards perfection, be sure to enjoy the simple things and take pride in their success. Doing this well will add an additional feather to your cap of confidence.

Celebrate Small Goals and Achievements

In the first step, we spoke about the importance of small goals. Be sure not to lose the habit of setting small goals. Besides, even a so-called big goal is a collection of small goals. Also, setting goals should not be a challenging task.

It is about having them, achieving them, and celebrating them. With time, this forms your success story.

Be in Control of Your World

Never at any moment let go of strong positive mental images. Make them the fuel to keep you on track of achieving your needed desire. Be sure to always tap into the tremendous potential that comes with positive thinking.

Besides, to develop confidence, you need to get better at handling failure. One of the things that sets a confident person apart is the fact that they own up to their mistakes and shortcomings, which is bound to happen when trying something new. Errors should be steps on the path towards progress.

Step 3: Gear Towards Success

Before getting to the third stage, you should have felt your confidence to lead building up. Many of the things you set your heart to in the previous step should already be done. Hence, there should be enough success to serve as motivation.

This is not a clue to stop but to keep going. Set bigger and harder goals and be sure to always be on your toes. Make more commitments and seek new areas to apply the skills you have learned.

Be sure not to allow overconfidence to eat you up. Resist the urge to take on a task in order to prove your capabilities to your followers.

Relentless and Unbeatable

Keep stretching yourself, but make sure you do it gradually. This is part of the building block you need to add to your wall of self-confidence.

The most essential skill you need to improve to gain more confidence to be a leader is setting goals, so make sure to utilize this tested skill.

Chapter 8:
How Navy SEALS Stay in Control in Any Situation

If you aspire to become more resilient or just extraordinary in everything you do, you must investigate the life of a Navy SEAL and learn from it. There is a wide range of lessons to learn from these people who are always ready to take on the toughest challenges whenever needed. Even though you do not intend to go through the same rigors as the SEALs, you may want to look out for the things that set them aside from other US Armed Forces and of course, Armed Forces across the globe.

In the past, several members of the elite group have shared their experience and knowledge of the ways people excelled beyond their physical prowess both at training camps and in the line of duty. Therefore, for everyone who wishes to improve, it is necessary to learn lessons from these special forces, follow their leads, and watch how much better they are going to become.

Mental Toughness and Resilience

Winston Churchill once advised that when you are going through hell, you should keep going. This is a very valuable piece of advice. Navy

Relentless and Unbeatable

SEALs are the toughest in the world because they have successfully walked through hell. This is because, over time, they have developed mental toughness. This is important for every aspect of life as it is a well-known/effective tool to achieve long-term success. All that matter is having the ability to keep going when the going gets extremely tough. You see, in today's world of smartphones, automated procedures, and artificial intelligence, people tend to chicken out at the slightest difficulty. Therefore, what sets one apart from the rest is one's ability to cultivate mental agility and resilience. This helps place one's head high up in the air to become a pacesetter/forerunner of another people's success

To create a state of mental toughness, the first step that SEALs goes through is a sort of mental segmentation. Imagining that they must eat an elephant, SEALs segment their challenge into parts so that they can gradually eat one part after the other. This works in real life scenarios, so whatever you are faced with, it is important to break it down into surmountable parts. Take marathoners for example; instead of creating a mental visualization of the entire race, they take it one lap at a time, slowing down and going faster when they should, and picking up all the strength left in them as they get close to the finish line. If they approached every single step of the race with the same energy, they would either be too exhausted to get the finish line, or too slow to get to it. In real life situations, when you have a mountain-sized task, break it down into smaller rocks and approach them one after the other. Avoid thinking of the task in its entirety as this may be discouraging. However, you should try to fit the segmented tasks into a 24-hour schedule.

Another technique employed by SEALs is to create a mental picture of success. This serves as self-motivation. By visualizing success, you sort of get a feel of what success is like. While at it, you are forced to envisage all the things you should do and all the steps you need to take to achieve this success. While doing so, make sure you put all your senses to work. Also, make sure your mental picture of success is as real as possible, as you do not want to build castles in the air. Try to not picture yourself failing as much as you can, and rather continuously picture yourself succeeding effortlessly. Think about the consequences of possible failure. You will not want to disappoint your loved one, so picture their faces as they hear the news of your failure. Also, consider the embarrassment that comes with failure, then play all these images in your head again from time to time until success is a reality. Whenever you must get through a difficult phase, think of what it will feel like to come out of it successfully, and use that as your motivating factor.

Talk Positively to Yourself

One of the characteristics of SEALS is the ability to stay calm in the face of danger. According to research, the brain is always active, and it is estimated to say about 300 to 1000 words per minute. To this effect, when you seem to be in the face of danger, the brain goes to work, suggesting an avalanche of 'how's' and 'what ifs. So, the good thing is that you can control what goes on in your head. Like the Navy SEAL, always make sure there is no room for negative thoughts in your head.

There are a whole lot of things that SEALs are not allowed to do, and one of them is to panic. Even when underwater and with their oxygen mask suddenly yanked off, instead of panicking, a SEAL works to find ways to restore the mask. When the brain goes into danger mode and wants to tell you that you are about to die, the mind of a Navy SEAL goes into positive thoughts and tells himself that survival is the only option, and that optimism is key. This is in sharp contrast to the mind of a pessimist. A pessimist always reminds himself of the magnitude of a problem and convinces himself that a bad situation is going to last forever, or perhaps that such situations are a universal phenomenon, like, "trust issues are universal; no one can be trusted". Also, they find fault in themselves in everything; "I am just not good at hiking". A Navy SEAL's mind sees positivity at all times; "Oh! This won't last forever, I'll overcome it", bad things are there are for a reason; "if I can't trust a person or people, it is for a reason" and finally, a SEAL doesn't fault himself for every failure; the fact that he was unable to complete a task is because he probably missed a step, not because he isn't good at it. When talking to yourself, it is important to rid your mind of all forms of pessimism. Remember that success is what you are in for, and negative thoughts drown you faster than you can imagine.

A SEAL constantly tells himself that so many people have passed the test in the past and those people are not better than them. Every minute of their training comes with rigorous mental and physical tests, so they constantly must give themselves positive talks to keep their eyes on the goal and to never give up. This can be you in every aspect of your life. Tests and trials will certainly come your way, but you always must tell yourself that you are not the worse off person in life. So, as the strongest among the many strong people alive, you will excel.

Control Your Emotions

There are times when our emotions seem to rush in like a flood and at such times, we are likely to lose control of all our senses. These emotions may be a result of stress and as soon as they hit, our major stress hormones - adrenaline, cortisol, and norepinephrine - provide us with a boost of energy. However, there is only so much these hormones can take. When they are elevated for a long period, it becomes impossible to switch to relaxation mode. Sleeping becomes a task, motivations fall to an all-time low, and the immune system has a tough time functioning. In such situations, the SEALs apply a solution known as 4 by 4 of 4. Here is how it works: breathe out for four seconds, breathe in for four seconds, then repeat it another four minutes.

Relentless and Unbeatable

This may look familiar as so many experts like yogis have been doing this for quite a long time. The truth is that our bodies have effects on our brains and vice versa. When the body is stressed, the brain sends signals that tell you to take some time off. It gets to a point where the brain literally shuts down as a result of stress. This simple breathing exercise helps you switch your stress hormones off and prepare the body for relaxation. When you get to the point of raging emotions, the best thing you can do is to stop everything you are doing. Remind yourself of the fact that you will not achieve much if your emotions are not right so as often as you can, take a moment off to do the 4 by 4 of 4. If you are having a bad day at work, pause, breathe and continue. Maybe you are an introvert that is faced with the herculean task of addressing a crowd. Once you get on that stage, it may seem like your tongue is stuck to the roof of your mouth. Well, you may not have the time to do the last four, but the first fours will certainly work magic in calming your nerves. Breathe in and out and notice how your tension eases.

Set Goals

At some point, all your muscles and nerves will scream at you to quit and will even threaten to break down if you don't. At such times, you need all the motivation you can get to keep going. Goals are very good motivating factors. Navy SEALs like to set achievable goals, which are sometimes small, but they are always enough to keep them going at tough times. For a Navy SEAL, during training, making it to the next minute may be a very difficult task as they have tons of hurdles to cross while the clock is ticking. Their small goals, however, could be to make it to lunch or dinner at the training camp so when they are underwater, they must keep reminding themselves that it is impossible to quit or die as they must eat lunch or dinner at the camp, not elsewhere, and certainly not as a dead man. This may be an extremely inconsequential phenomenon for the other man, but for the SEAL, it is important to keep him going. When they achieve their goals, they set new ones which are often a step ahead of the former. The goal is to keep improving and keep getting better.

For you, these goals are also very important. Keep a note of the things you want to achieve and make sure you don't relent until you achieve them. Track your success as there is no better motivation than seeing yourself succeed. Like the Navy SEAL, when you have achieved a goal, set your sights higher by setting new ones. Make sure you prepare yourself to achieve your goals by creating a visual picture of the journey towards achieving these goals.

Visualization

The task ahead of you may seem so humongous that you may already have some doubts about it. Well, since it is ahead, you may not know what it feels like now, but you can prepare yourself to know what to expect and what not to. This will be made easy by simply creating a mental picture of the whole process. This way, you will have already envisaged the possible twists and turns that you are most likely to encounter. As you are creating this picture, make room for eventualities so that you are not thrown off your feet at any point while carrying out the task. This can be done by simply closing your eyes and meditating for a few minutes. Picture what is ahead of you, then walk yourself through each step of it. It may sound silly, but the best of the best does it and it absolutely works. SEALs are taught to do this a lot by having a mental rehearsal of the activities that are to come, then visualizing themselves succeeding in those activities. However, be careful not to merely fantasize about these things because this will mean that you will not see any obstacles in your journey. Bring the possible obstacles into the picture and visualize yourself surpassing them. Fantasies are a known killer of motivation as they do not really give you the energy you need to undertake the task ahead of you. After forming a mental picture of your task, you must find ways to take it to the next level like a professional, and that brings us to the next technique:

Make Use of Simulations

While it is a great idea to visualize the task ahead, it is equally good to take some mock exercises to align yourself with the things you are going to undergo. The good thing about visualization is that is very mobile, so you can do it anywhere and everywhere.

It has been discovered that SEALs don't just visualize. It has been said that before the Navy SEALs raided Osama Bin-Laden's house, they created replicas of the location, so their training was tailored towards the things they were likely to face. Like the US Navy SEAL team 6 on the 11th of May 2011, you too can create mental simulations of the exercises ahead of you. If you are going to have a presentation, for example, create a small supportive group and practice in front of them. If according to your mental picture, you are going to answer questions from members of your audience, ask those in your small group to ask you tough questions. Treat those questions as the real deal and answer them as though your success depends on it. This way, you will have gotten yourself acquainted with most parts of your exercise.

Think of Small Victories

Some days can be so bad that it feels like everything is going wrong. Remember, the power of positive thoughts will give you more strength than you may be able to sum up on your own. However, on the days where you seem to be losing it, what you are expected to do is to think of those small but highly consequential victories of yours.

The day may have started off as every other day, but you stepped out of the house and realized that you must have lost your wallet. To make things worse, it suddenly began to rain and now, your phone is drenched in water. Also, you got to work late and now, you are going to get queried. Well, how worse could your day have gone? Maybe it is time to look at the bright side and think about the days when you were the champion of your workplace because you single-handedly completed a task that shaped the fate of the entire company. Remind yourself of the fact that you are still that champion and that the bad day is only temporary. Tomorrow is just another day to show off your greatness. You may also want to think smaller; maybe the office scenario is not for you, depending on what you do. Now, think of the times you said a joke that made everyone laugh; maybe it is time to be your own savior by telling yourself the same joke or even more, to win a smile. Also, you could think about the many times you made your daughter's day by buying her candy on your way home from work. Picture her reaction - does it warm your heart? Maybe it is time to get another heart-melting reaction from your darling little daughter. We know you have lost your wallet but what greater victory is there than to go out of your way to make the one that means so much to you happy? Think of how happy you will be to make her happy. To Navy SEALs, this is another way to get themselves to keep moving in the race of life that seems to be filled with perpetual adversaries.

The thought of small victories lifts one's morale and high morale will propel you to push forward to even higher morale. This is basically the stepping stone to victory, so if you seem to be having a not so pleasant day, you should consider your small wins instead of counting the big losses.

Stay Away from Bad Stuff
The fact that Navy SEALs undergo the toughest training in the US military makes them qualified to take on anyone at any time. It also means that they stand tall as one of the most prestigious arms of the

US military. However, this does not mean that they are ready to take up arms at the slightest provocation. Navy SEALs are thought to avoid bad situations before they happen until fighting becomes inevitable. People generally think that a SEAL's first reaction would be to take up arms. This is untrue. They only use their arms as a last resort. This is a very potent technique that should be applied to everyone's dealings. Try to avoid bad situations as much as possible, no matter how strong you may think you are. Even though you may have what it takes to handle the situation, if it is bad, avoid it as much as you can. You should not waste your time around bad vibes that can be avoided.

Be Humble

As strong as Navy SEALs are, they are a humble lot and in so many cases, as already explained with the previous technique, they learn not to wield their strength. A SEAL team leader is said to always recognize the fact that he is not the solution to every problem. Once he begins to place himself in front of every problem, he is said to be heading towards failure. It is against this background that delegation comes in. Also, they are humble enough to accept their faults when things go wrong, to accept constructive criticism, to listen when they should and call for help when it is necessary. This does not mean they are weak, and it doesn't diminish their leadership status; if anything, it makes them better leaders. Humility is a technique that has built successful leaders across all walks of life. Certainly, this technique is not restricted to leaders alone. Followers also always need to be humble enough to know and accept their position. You never want to rub shoulders with your superiors or anyone at all in whatever situation, so humility always comes in handy. This is a great way to eliminate stress.

Box Breathing

This technique called box breathing works to keep you cool and it is called that way because it has four simple steps, each in four seconds (a square). This technique can be practiced anytime and anywhere you feel the need to relax, whether you are on a battlefront, in an exam hall, at a seminar, or simply reading a tweet. It only takes sixteen seconds to complete one circle and you can keep repeating it until you feel relaxed. For the SEAL, on the other hand, it is advised to do this technique for five minutes. Here is a step by step rundown of this technique:

Breathe in for four seconds: you are expected to expel every atom of air from your lungs before you breathe in. Once done, begin to inhale and make sure you take in all the air you can to fill your lungs to their full capacity.

Hold your breath for another four seconds - at this point, you are no longer expected to take in any air, and you must ensure that no air escapes from your lungs.

Exhale for four seconds: now, gradually expel the air from your lungs for four seconds. Make sure you can get all the air out of your lungs.

Leave your lungs empty for four seconds - you may be tempted to inhale right after you let out all the air from your lungs, but please don't. Wait another four seconds before you take in air again.

Just like the 4 by 4 for 4, this is just another technique that will work perfectly to keep you calm in the face of great trouble. Give it a try.

Find the Most Important Moment

In SEAL training, one of the toughest routines is training to attack enemy ships. During this training, a candidate is left underwater on his own and must swim to attack an enemy ship. The ship is built in a way where you get no light from the moon or from any nearby street lights, and ambient lights are also blocked. They are simply left in the dark with their instinct to go and attack a ship by themselves, approaching it from the bottom. The candidate is meant to go under the ship to find the center line and the deepest part of the ship. The most difficult part of the mission is described by some that have passed through the training, as the darkest part. However, it is also seen as the most important part, so it is very important to get everything right to know when and how to strike. These phases exist in everyone's life and like the Navy SEAL, it is important to not only strike at the right time but to also not miss the catch.

Be Aware of your Surroundings

This might come off as a very basic technique but thanks to mobile devices and gadgets, that is not the case anymore. Being aware of

Relentless and Unbeatable

one's surrounding is another way in which SEALs can excel. Once you step into an environment, take note of the tiny little details so that you know when something changes. Any change at all may be a sign of possible danger so in order not to be caught unaware, Navy SEALs are trained to always be alert by knowing their surroundings. Whether in an office or in a public place, try to get your head up from your computer or mobile phone and study what is going on around you. You may notice that everyone has suddenly gone quiet or that people are suddenly beginning to avoid some things. Asides from people, you may also find out that the position of a thing has changed, or a part of the room has become cooler than it used to be. Knowing the reason for these changes will be enough to tell you to either run or stay. This is a very simple technique that you should imbibe.

Chapter 9:
How the Extraordinary Stay Extraordinary

Reading this book indicates that you are interested in mental toughness, but let me ask you this, do you really know what it is, what it entails, and what it requires? Some people are born with this mental toughness while some are not, so they will need to work harder to develop it. The good thing about mental toughness is that there are things you can do to improve it, but are you ready for it?

Getting ready for mental toughness is a common challenge faced by a lot of athletes of all sports, parents, performers, and coaches. Fully developing your mental strength requires a lot of skills training which is the key to achieving the goals set before you, and this training is always where we find it difficult to keep up; we might get stuck and give up in the process and end up going back to where we started.

The truth is, training your mental strength to its full potential will benefit you when you put more work to it. But how do you develop this mental strength? First, let us define what mental toughness is.

What Is Mental Toughness?

Now, for easier understanding, I will define mental toughness in two parts:

Mental toughness is the ability to get into a certain zone of action and as a reward for doing that, your performance gets to its peak when you need it the most.

Also, it is the grit or resilience that you use to push through the adversity you are facing in order to achieve success.

Mental toughness is often associated with sportsmen, but it applies to life in general and developing it would do everyone a great deal of good.

Is Mental Toughness Important?

Maybe you are already in the process of training for your mental process, or you are about to embark in the journey towards this and want to take a step back because are beginning to doubt whether it is important for you. Well, the obvious truth is that building your mental toughness can help you separate the good from the great.

Have you ever asked yourself why the world's top performers always retain their titles and take the trophies home? Can you figure out why they are always winners and wouldn't want to give room for any kind of mistakes as they always try to achieve their goals?

If you have asked yourself this before, you are not alone. I have studied and even worked with different sportsmen from different parts of the world and they all have the same secret to winning. They all state that mental toughness is critical in order to win.

Let's create a scenario here: you are taking part in a very important competition and you begin to choke of fear, and anxiety walks in, you get scared and switch to a zone where you are not supposed to be. To take on such a competition, you need enough mental toughness.

As a sportsman, the first rule of sports psychology is that you need mental toughness to achieve top performance. Getting mentally tough is not about your physical abilities. Successfully getting mentally tough borders on changing how you think. It requires an everyday discipline and a daily effort.

The greatest challenge faced by individuals that want to achieve mental toughness is that they tend to dwell in the past and never progress on their journey to becoming mentally tough. Humans are bound to go through changes all the time and sometimes, these may be positive changes, but it happens to everyone, even those that seem to be doing very well at the highest levels

Getting mentally tough will make you uncomfortable, but the discomfort is an important piece that will help you build your mental toughness. Whether you are a sportsman, a SEAL candidate, a business professional, or anything else, you will have to go through this discomfort in order to achieve that toughness, but at the end of the day, it is all worth it. Now, you know how important mental toughness is to become a winner.

The 5 Steps to Developing Mental Strength

After doing lots of research, reading quite several memoirs from different ex-SEALS, and speaking to a handful of world winners, I have come to realize that building mental toughness requires work and there are steps to take in order to achieve this.

I have carefully taken the time to put these simple techniques down, and they have been proven to work for a lot of people. Now, the question is - are you ready? If you are, read on to learn simple techniques that will help you build your mental toughness.

Each technique I have written here comes with an explanation and a practical application to a person's real life.

Step 1: Take the Bull by the Horn; Take Little Steps

If you are asking yourself how the hell you are going to take a bull by the horn, well, we don't mean this literally. It means getting involved one step at a time without letting distractions in. When you are faced with a daunting task like a marathon with many competitors beside you, you can get scared, feel that fear, and end up stopping before you even start, and you don't want that.

As a sportsman, the solution to this fear is segmentation. You should slowly divide your tasks into more workable parts by taking your challenges one step at a time. I know you might have often heard the cliché saying, "one step at a time", but it always works, so why not try it?

This technique is employed by many triathletes and ultra-marathoners. They focus on their immediate objective, the next point of achievement, and block all distractions throughout the entire race.

Application: You should break your daunting tasks into immediate little goals. In order to make it less stressful and boring, they should preferably fit in a few hours. When you do this, focus on completing each part one at a time instead of facing all tasks at once.

This technique should help you attempt the task instead of getting overwhelmed with the fear of the unknown and eventually avoiding it.

Step 2: Focused Visualization

You might be wondering how you can picture success when you are not successful yet. Well, you will get the answer to this question after reading all about this technique and you will know that it will help a great deal in building your mental toughness.

A footballer always imagines scoring a goal before he eventually scores it, and a basketballer will visualize free throws and will later find out that his mental picture of the free throw was somewhat accurate, after making the basket. Why not create that illusion? Why not see yourself doing it? Why not make visualizations come to reality?

I have come to realize that good visualization gives people the following qualities:

- Detailed, vivid, and sharp senses.
- The actualization of your imagination.

Positive imagery

By now, you should know that the secret to happiness is success as it brings happiness along with it. Achieving success involves using the full power of our minds. Since our mind has the power to create and destroy forces of the world, we should use it to our advantage. You can use it to create wonderful things you have dreamed of, but also to take it all away.

If you haven't been making use of visualization, it can be simple for you to get your hands on it, but it can prove daunting too. The question now is; how do you know what you are doing is visualizing or how do you get it right? At one point or the other, you might have been involved in the use of imagination to fantasize about what you like. When you were a kid, you used your imaginary power to daydream about how you would like your future to be, as well as other things.

You should now have a clear picture of what imagination entails and how you can use it. Not everyone can see through their mind's eye but if you can do this, you are at an advantage because imagination comes with its benefits.

If a high-rated Navy SEAL is quietly sitting in the corner of a room before his mission, what do you think he is imagining while seated? The success of his mission or fear of failure? Well, what he is doing there is called focused visualization. This visualization is called focused because it can be controlled, empowered, and fixed at a specific target.

Now, we will be looking at two forms of focused visualization that will help you build your mental toughness as you go.

Performance Imagery
Performance imagery is a form of focused visualization that can be used to develop mental strength for a mission or skill set. If you want to embark on a mission, visualize your plan on how to get your target and keep going over the plan in your mind's eye. You can slow things down in order to make sure you are using the right technique and to ensure it is effective in battle.

Using this technique will allow you to analyze errors and correct them, maintain your skills, increase your confidence, improve your techniques, and simulate your various alternative responses.

When practicing the performance imagery technique, you can add subtle body movements with your eyes closed - this will strengthen the connection between the mind and body and allow the internal visualization to be more prevailing.

Future Imagery

Sometimes, how you see yourself is different from how others see you, whether positively or negatively. However, what if I told you that there was a way to hold a powerful image of who you would like to be in the present as well as in the future?

As a Navy Seal, black belt, senator or firefighter, if you can support your mental vision with action, take away negativity, and fuel what you have envisioned with strong belief, desire, and expectation, you will get to where you want to be.

Another way to use your imagination is to imagine what failure feels like. Imagine what the consequences will be when you fail. Imagine what the faces of your friends and family will look like when they hear that you have failed. Imagine the pain from the embarrassment you would be facing if that happened and feel every inch of it.

Application: When you embark on a huge and stressful event, use your imagination to imagine your success as well as the pain of failing.

Step 3: Controlling Your Emotions

When your body is going through great stress, a surge in the body's main stress hormones (cortisol, adrenaline, and norepinephrine) will give you a boost of focus and energy. However, if the stress hormones stay at a high surge for a long time, switching to relaxation mode becomes difficult. You will then be faced with sleeping troubles, motivation tumbles, and problems in your immune system.

Breath Control Exercises

Controlling your breath is not limited to controlling arousal; it can also be used to change your state of mind when you are deeply stressed. Navy SEALS and athletes use this technique to control their breath to prepare for a mission or event.

Breath control exercises entail psyching yourself mentally and physically by using deep diaphragmatic breathing, powerful visualization, forced exhalations, and powerful affirmations.

Deep Diaphragmatic Breathing

When you breathe, it happens consciously and unconsciously. Unconscious breathing is referred to as "chest breathing"; it requires energy as it is labor intensive. Chest breathing will lower your energy storage and increase your anxiety.

When you are faced with a difficult mission and are feeling stressed, use the deep diaphragmatic breathing pattern.

Relentless and Unbeatable

You can use this pattern by disciplining yourself with "box breathing". This should be done in a quiet environment.

To use "box breathing", you should inhale and count to 5, hold your breath and count to 5, then exhale and again count to 5. You can do it again or count to 4 if getting to 5 is a little difficult. Now, in four smooth counts, exhale the air that you inhaled, through the nose.

Simple, right? This is closely related to yoga as yogis have been doing this for a very long time now. This method has proven to always be effective and is therefore extremely helpful.

What happens to your brain affects your body, and the other way around too, so use this simple breathing exercise to control your emotions by switching your stress hormones off and preparing the body for relaxation mode.

Let's look at the advantages of using deep diaphragmatic box breathing:

- Controls arousal response.
- Reduces performance anxiety.
- Increases brain performance.
- Increases focus and attention.

Relaxation Breath

This method can be used when in action. Since it is impossible to hold your breath when you are on a mission, using the relaxation breathing technique can help you instead.

To do this, you can drop the part where you hold your breath and just inhale, count to 5 starting from your diaphragm and fill up the middle of your chest as if you are gulping in air, then immediately start exhaling. You can repeat this process again.

This relaxation technique is important as it helps you control your arousal response in order to remain present, in control, and focused. If you keep practicing it, it will eventually become part of you and will become a natural breathing state that provides you with both physical and mental benefits.

Application: If you are already into meditation, this will be of great help. So, the next time you are stressed, take a break with deep breaths before continuing the rest of your day.

Step 4: Mental Stability

As humans, we are all emotional creatures that can easily be affected by things around us or comments about us. In this type of situation, your emotion is at work, and this is where your mental stability comes in.

Just like any other mental skill, your mental stability can be trained to strengthen your general mental health. For this to happen, observe your reaction towards a negative comment, thoughts or events, and keep a tab on how you allow those external factors to get to you and ruin your day.

It is always difficult to keep your cool especially when the closest people to you are driving you nuts. You start getting upset because you feel like they should be the least people offending you.

It isn't bad to expect happiness from your loved ones, so it is totally normal to be upset when they hurt you. However, remember that every time you are upset, it is your fault because you set expectations for them.

The truth is, people are so engrossed in things and don't always think of what they say to you, as well as the consequences of their words. They might not even know their words hurt, so they haven't upset you intentionally. Everyone strives to behave in the best way possible, but our imperfection always sells us out - at one point, we make mistakes. Some people might realize their mistakes while others won't but whatever the case may be, you shouldn't hold grudges or let it get to you.

Their actions towards you might be due to what they are going through - maybe they are having issues at school or work. Always give people around you the benefit of the doubt so that you can make peace with yourself. Show empathy and always put yourself in their shoes. At the end of the day, most of these things wouldn't even matter because you will always forgive yourself for feeling hurt, so why not immediately forgive others and move on?

In order to have that mental stability, you need to stop blaming people around you and instead own up and take full responsibility for expecting too much from people. If someone does not meet your expectations, drop those expectations, and if someone does better than you expected, be appreciative. However, no one owes it to you to behave nicely, so whatever happens, embrace it and move on.

This can also be applied to life. Life owes us nothing when it is good, so be thankful, and when it is bad, don't get sucked in and remain where you are, and dust the negativity off and move on. Use this opportunity to train your mind to be at peace with whatever comes.

Several things can be linked to your mood change, but the origin remains the same. Whatever it may be, identify the cause, modify your reaction, and look at the positive side.

Step 5: Set Goals Aligned with Your Purpose
A lot of people think that you need to work hard to succeed. Undoubtedly, success requires hard work, but you should also know that succeeding doesn't require you to suffer and go through lots of struggle. Succeeding can be done effortlessly, without having to stress yourself too much. So, in a way, you can have fun while succeeding.

Relentless and Unbeatable

A great way to succeed without having to go through unnecessary suffering or working harder than you should is to choose the right goal for you. When your goals are aligned with your purpose, working hard will become fun and you will steadily and easily achieve success.

The goals you set for yourself need to relate to your ethos or should be able to define your purpose in life. Many times, people set goals that don't have a connection to their ethos and when time passes, they start asking themselves what they are doing.

The goals you set should be able to meet up to the challenges in order to never make quitting an option when the going gets tough.

The above techniques should be practiced daily for you to train and develop your mental strength to make it that of an elite warrior.

Chapter 10:
Anti-Habits Holding You Back from Your True Potential

Breaking off bad habits isn't just about stopping them but also about substituting them with other meaningful things. It is always easy to separate the bad from the good, but since you know it is bad, why do you keep doing it? Everyone has the tendency to develop a bad habit but the ability to control it is what differentiate you from others.

Some bad habits are minor, like constantly leaving all your dirty dishes on the table or leaving your clothes on the sofa, while some habits can be worse like being addicted to watching porn, drinking excessive alcohol, and smoking which can affect your health in the long run.

If you feel that you have a habit that is controlling you - this is bad, and you should try to break it and set yourself free. Fighting bad habits is always difficult when you don't have a replacement for it. When you try stopping the habit and become idle, you might just fall back to that bad habit.

It is difficult to break a bad habit is because it has been rooted in your mind due to the constant repetition of the act, especially when it comes to a pleasurable act. The pleasure that it comes with will only get the brain fired up and this will continue even when you stop the habit, as you will now be left struggling with cravings for it. Your ability to control your emotions will determine whether you move past the habit or go back to it.

How Did You Develop Bad Habits?

In order to break free from bad habits, you should know how it became a habit. Habits are a pattern of behavior that started as something insignificant, but when you consciously or unconsciously repeat this behavior, it turns into a habit.

Breaking free from the patterns of this behavior will help you break free from the habits too. Normally, there is a trigger to every pattern, and this trigger can be emotional, environmental, or situational. The emotional trigger is attached to being addicted to drinking and smoking, while an environmental or situational trigger is when you see the dishwasher and a bunch of dirty plates but still decide to leave it for a later time as you still have one clean dish.

This autopilot behavior can be practical to you. When it triggers, it keeps you from re-inventing the normal routine of your daily lives and allows you to make infinite numbers of decisions daily, as well as provides you with enough brain-space to think about other things.

However, the disadvantage of the routine pattern is that it creates more trouble than good.

Easy Steps to Break A Bad Habit

The key to breaking bad habits is becoming aware and identifying them without any form of judgment. Once you have this covered, the next thing to do is to follow the steps to help you break free from it. The reason why you need to become fully aware of this is that when you eventually stop the habit and there is a trigger in your brain that wants you to go back to it, you will be fully aware and know it isn't good for you - just like a reminder.

So, if you have bad habits that you want to break free from, here are some steps to help you get started:

Identify the Triggers

Having so many plates in the kitchen is enough trigger to make you pile up dirty plates because you are made to think that you have not exhausted all the plates in your kitchen yet. Also, the sight of the refrigerator may be a reminder of the fact that there is alcohol in the fridge, ready for you to take. Identifying these triggers means that there is a way for you to push back and not allow the trigger to get a hold of you.

A lot of people are faced with the difficulty of identifying their triggers and when this happens, you can work it out by going backward. For example, if you see your fridge and are really craving a drink, you should slow down and use the responsiveness to this behavior as a signal to ask yourself why you are acting in an uncontrollable manner or what is emotionally wrong with you - that is the trigger you have identified.

Deal with The Triggers

Since you have identified the triggers, the next thing to do is to break loose from that pattern. Here, you should deliberately reduce the number of plates you have in your kitchen or if it is a beer addiction, you should try to reduce the number of beers in your fridge.

Instead of responding to the danger of the triggers, you can do other deliberate things in order to get your mind off the habit, such as engaging in deep breathing to relax your mind when the trigger sets in.

Change the Larger Pattern

Here, the context surrounding your habit-pattern will be explored. For example, you leave your dishes dirty because you still have some clean ones that you can use, or you drink a lot of beer after work because you believe it makes you feel more relaxed. So, you need to start by cleaning up your dirty dishes because you will still have to be the one to do them, and it will ultimately be unavoidable.

When you look at it and change your pattern, you make it easy to tackle the habit and practice putting your willpower in place.

Use Prompts

Using prompts is like a reminder to help you break the pattern by making use of your positive triggers. This will alert you and help you stay on track. Instead of leaving them on the dining table or wherever you used them, try placing your dirty plates on the sink where you can see them, or you even can set a reminder on your phone to alert you when to clean them.

Stop Doing Them

This is obvious. If you want to end a bad habit and swap it with something more meaningful and productive, then it is only right to stop the bad habit. If the habit is not helping you in any way, why are you still doing it?

Develop A Substitute Plan

As mentioned earlier, breaking loose from bad habits isn't all about stopping as it also involves substituting the habit with something else.

How do you stop drinking when you are with friends that drink? Or, how can you manage not to drink at a party where everyone is drinking? You can substitute your beer drinking habit and grab a mocktail instead and hang out with people that you can make conversation with instead of giving in to the beer trigger.

If you want to avoid getting tempted to smoke, you can substitute it with eating your favorite snack or if you are addicted to porn, you can help yourself by getting a book to read when you feel bored or even going out with friends in order to take your mind off it.

This trigger will always present itself and it can kick in at any time but if you are ready to get rid of your bad habit, you need to set a new direction for yourself. Instead of indulging in a habit that will only bring you pain and regret, you can do other fun stuff like exercise, read a book, or even meditate.

Attach A Bigger Purpose Behind Your Change

People decide that they want to cut off a habit because it is believed to be a bad habit and the right thing to do is to get rid of it. Instead of saying it is the right thing to do, why not say it is an absolute must to get rid of it? This will show your readiness and help keep the triggers at bay.

Now, you can only see the bigger purpose if you can answer the following questions - why do you want to get rid of the habit? Is it really a bad habit? Has it been affecting your progress? Will your life be better off without it?

Once you can answer these questions and come to the realization that the habit is bad and that you need to get rid of it, it's time to attach it to a bigger purpose.

Perhaps drinking too many beers is beginning to affect your health and it's showing, or you are addicted to watching porn and it's affecting your relationship and your mental health; so, why not make a huge difference by using that energy for a bigger purpose?

You can put this energy towards a skill you have always wanted to acquire but haven't found the time to, or even a side business you've always wanted to run. The bad habit does not serve a bigger purpose, so why not add more fuel to your change and focus on bigger things?

Get Support

When it proves difficult to curtail the habit or to stay in control, you can seek support from a friend. Get support from someone you can easily call, talk to, or get motivation from when the cravings kick in. A close friend can be very helpful, especially one that doesn't have the bad habits that you are trying to push aside.

You can hang out with your buddy and grab a cup of coffee instead of drinking beer. Spend time together, talk, and express how you feel, as this will help you.

However, if you have really done your best and still can't overcome the habit, it is time to seek professional help. This can be a doctor that will prescribe the right medication for you because the habit has become chronic and risks being a disorder.

Another way to go about this is to see a therapist that will not only help you work on the source and trigger of your habits but will also give you the necessary support that you need.

All bad habits are not the same or created equally but they all have an all-encompassing goal which is to give you a setback. Take charge of your life, be more proactive, and be deliberate in everything you do.

Stay Consistent

When you are looking at leaving those bad habits behind you for good, consistency is key. It took time for the bad habit to root and plant itself in your brain, so it will take time for it to be uprooted and replaced with another habit.

The strategy to go with is consistency. You must stay consistent with the new habit and engage with it more. The more you engage with it, the more your brain registers and adapts to it. Your brain will get wired around it and it will become easier to trigger the new habit than the bad one.

If you want to stop drinking beer, substitute it with another drink and as you start to drink it often, your brain will register it due to consistency.

Chapter 11:
Why Losers Never Get Better

Why do you need to win? Why do people lose? How do you win? What are the differences between a winner and a loser?

These are essential questions that you need to know the answer to. By nature, humans are very competitive, with an exaggerated sense of self-importance. We always want to prove we are just a little better than others or even than our own selves. We can't help ourselves from competing; in fact, in this world, we compete for almost everything. That is the dividing line between "winners" and "losers".

Why Do You Need to Win?

When you have a goal and want to achieve it, it will naturally lead to competition. At some point, your greatest competitor is yourself and for you to be victorious, you must first conquer the old you. Some goals are simple, and due to the surrounding circumstances, they are easy to achieve. Other goals may be extremely difficult, and to achieve them, you will need a lot of hard work, dedication, and a powerful mental state to attain victory and be successful.

Everyone needs to be a winner at some point to prove to themselves and their surroundings that they don't just exist but are truly alive.

Then Why Do People Lose?
Because they fail to achieve the desired outcome of their initial goal and fail to try again and again.

"I've missed more than 9000 shots in my career. I've lost almost 300 games. 26 times, I've been trusted to take the game winning shot and missed. I've failed over and repeatedly in my life. And that is why I succeed". - Michael Jordan

How Do You Win?
Just like the quote above, failing doesn't mean that you have lost. Losing is when you stop trying to improve on what you did wrong. When you are determined to work on your set goal, take solid action until you achieve the result that you aimed for. The continuous actions that you have taken express your attitude towards success.

What Are the Differences Between A Winner and A Loser?
There has never been a real competition between a winner and a loser. At times, it may seem like people are just destined to succeed and win at every turn and progress unhindered, while others stagnate and can't accomplish anything. The dividing line between these two people is down to their attitudes and habits.

Most people with success stories usually have a long history of failures, but that doesn't mean they are losers. Yes! They have failed several times, but with the right attitude, mindset, habits, and actions, they persist until they achieve success.

The mindset of every individual can influence and determine if they are a winner or a loser. Let's look at some of the differences between the winner and the loser's mindset and understand what separates them.

Winners

- Winners will admit their mistakes, learn from them and try to improve.

- When there is a challenge, winners focus on the solutions.

- Winners will work hard whether someone is watching or not, as they are self-motivated.

- Winners set goals.

- Winners are consistent; they understand that the best way to achieve the desired successful outcome is consistency.

- Winners change strategies and explore other options when the initial plan is not working.

- Winners understand that when they fail, it is also a learning process, and it is treated as a learning experience on the road to success.

- Winners understand the influence of the people that surround them, so they surround themselves with people who can bring the best out of them.

- Winners are people who give back.

- Winners don't dwell in their comfort zone; they constantly seek to expand their boundaries.

- Winners have the mindset of "I must do something".

- Winners will put forth the maximum amount of effort when they take on any task.

Losers

- Losers will blame others for their mistakes and make excuses.

- Losers focus on problems.

- Losers will avoid work; they will only do what's needed for them to get by unless there's someone keeping an eye on them.

- Losers will expect to see and achieve results they desire and want to see the outcome overnight.

- Losers are afraid of setting goals.

- Losers keep repeating the same thing they did that didn't work repeatedly, expecting a different result.

- Losers are easily overwhelmed and tend to give up immediately as they are met with rejection or any form of failure.

- Losers will usually surround themselves with like-minded losers.

- Losers stay within the boundaries of their comfort zone.

- Losers have the philosophy of taking more and giving less or even giving nothing at all.

- Losers will say, "Something must be done"

- Losers will put in the least amount of effort required to meet the minimum criteria on a task.

7 Qualities That Define A Winner

1. Only Set Clearly Defined Goals
If you want to achieve reasonable results in anything you do, you first need to clearly define your goals. Someone without clearly defined goals is like a sailor without a navigating compass. When you set definite goals, it's like a compass that guides you towards a certain direction.

Relentless and Unbeatable

In order to win, you must be SMART in setting your goals. The SMART goal means:

Specific: you have a target area you want to work on.

Measurable: your goals are quantifiable, measurable, or can be gauged or viewed to take a certain dimension.

Assignable: your goals should be assignable, and you should be able to decide the place of a certain thing in the bigger picture where something belongs in a general scheme and who will do the task

Realistic: make sure that your goals are achievable and doable. Imagine setting a goal of counting the hairs on your head, which is totally unrealistic. Set goals that can be done within a period.

Time-bound: when your goals have a timeframe, it will unconsciously trigger the mental alarm that will drive you to achieve your goals within that time limit. Long goals without a time limit might lead to developing the habit of procrastination.

This acronym will enable you to turn your desired goals into normal habits and achieve success.

2. Self-Projection
What is self-projection? It simply means that you have a vivid and clear picture of your goals and what you really want to achieve.

Self-projection is basically knowing what your end goal should look like and keeping it in mind. But to winners, self-projection is much more than just knowing your end goal. It requires life and mental animation, so you can imagine a movie and play the scenes in your head, where you are the lead role in achieving that goal.

For example, if you want to climb a mountain, you can visualize the mountain climb you are planning, and you can see yourself climbing, sweating, overcoming challenges, and conquering the tasks nature has set for you. Having a solid and vivid view of your goals be a form of mental affirmation and will increase excitement.

3. Play to Win and Stay Positive

Losers are people who always worry. Instead of playing to win, they play not to lose. A loser will say "what if I'm not doing it right" while a winner will say "I believe I am doing it right". They go in with a positive mental attitude as well as the confidence to get it right.

When you find yourself using "What ifs", like "What if I don't hit the target when I shoot?" "What if I fail at my task?", "What if the boss hates me?", you are displaying the attitude of a loser.

Nothing good comes out of the excessive fear of losing; you will only worry yourself and become stressed and ultimately end up achieving nothing. Also, you will likely miss out on opportunities, fail at your tasks, or fail to accomplish your set goals.

Visualize yourself winning and see yourself achieving your goals. Replace all the "what ifs" with positive thoughts and an optimistic mindset.

4. Be Active and Not Passive (Self-Determination)

When you are taking on any task, be actively involved and own that project, and at that moment, make it your set goal. Visualize yourself successfully completing the project. Act passively, and don't do it just because your boss wants you to.

Winning and losing are all within your control, and if you take charge, you are directly controlling and directing the flow of success towards you. It means you have taken matters into your own hands and have not left it to fate because you are a self-determined person.

As a self-determined person, you influence things to work and happen according to your tactics, and you make sure nothing keeps you from achieving your goals. Winners change strategies and explore other options, and when their initial plan is not working, they always have a plan B.

When you are passive and have the mindset of a loser, you naturally "let things occur" while you just watch.

5. Self-Awareness

Winning or being a winner does not mean that you should be perfect, and it does not mean that you should use any means necessary to succeed without caring about the consequences.

It should be about understanding that you are not perfect and identifying your weaknesses to make plans to fix them. One quality of a winner is knowing the right thing at the right time. Also, to succeed, you don't have to do everything by yourself. Learn when to delegate tasks and outsource those that require a professional.

Focus on what you are good that and let others who are better than you at other aspects handle those. That way, you get things done quicker and you still win. It is all about knowing and understanding yourself.

Once you are self-aware, you can easily empathize with others. If you can feel and understand what those around you feel, you will have a broader understanding and know when to act and when not to.

When you understand yourself, you can understand others better as well; self-awareness can make you more adaptable to sudden changes, your adaptability will help you adjust on-the-go, and the chances that your set goals crash and fail due to sudden changes will be very low, so you will always be on track to succeed.

6. Self-Discipline

Most people would rather take the easy way out because no one really likes the fact that success requires a lot of work. Since we are in the real world, there are no hacks, shortcuts, or cheat codes.

To be successful, you must start from the very beginning, from the setting of goals to the planning and execution phases. To achieve all those, you need to build and maintain the habits that will lead you to your goals. One of these habits is self-discipline, where you set goals and see them through to the end, no matter what.

If you are a procrastinator, one of the ways to counter it is to incorporate self-discipline in your routine to keep you going.

7. Live in The Present

If you dwell in the past, your future will be foggy because you are compromising your present and have forgotten the value of time.

Once the past is gone, leave it in the past because you have the present where you can try repeatedly. The past should be viewed as a reference book that you learn from; you can consult it and learn from your past mistakes, but don't remain and wallow in the past.

All winners aim for the future by setting up SMART goals and acting upon them. Their projections cover years into the future, and they imagine how secure it will be. It will do you no good to set future goals and daydream all day about how the future will turn out or what it could hold and counting your future successes without acting. What you need today is the present because without it, you will have a compromised future with no success.

Winners take immediate action and work with the present, consult with the past, and project for the future. They plan time efficiently and have enough to spend with their family and loved ones.

5 Habits to Give Up If You Want to Be Successful

Some people have given up on pursuing their aspirations because they feel that their efforts will be in vain. They believe that it is their fault for not being successful in all their endeavors, they don't consider themselves intelligent, and therefore, their growth will be determined by fate.

What you should know and understand is that being successful cannot be hindered because you are not the most talented or brilliant; however, bad habits can do so. The following are 5 toxic habits that you quickly need to get rid of if you want to be successful.

Habit 1: Leave Your Comfort Zone

When you feel things are stagnated and you are just living your life on a repeat, it is time to explore new grounds, expand your horizon, and make new experiences. Whatever you do, don't just remain where you were; if you must crawl, do so and leave your comfort zone.

If you are performing the same job daily, reliving the same morning habits and ending up the night the same way, as well as have the same set of friends and same experiences, it is time to stop living the same month or year over and over, because you can't keep using the same strategy and expect different results.

You need to mix up daily routine, friends, and habits by changing your environment, creating new challenges, and finding new opportunities. Just leave your comfort zone as often as you can and experience new things, as variety is often said to be the spice of life.

Try thinking differently; take up a new hobby, do a road trip, sign up to take a class, or even teach one. Just challenge yourself, your body and your mind.

Habit 2: Pressure of People's Expectations of You

When you worry too much about people's opinion of you, you will have a tough time succeeding at many things. Your family, co-workers, boss, and boyfriend/girlfriend are all different individuals and will never know exactly how it feels to be you.

Allowing the expectations of others to weigh you down will only place you in a position where all you do is satisfy their expectations of you. If you fail to meet up to their expectations, it might lead to them having bad opinion of you, as well as ruining your connections and important relationships with them.

You need to stop letting the opinions and the expectations of others dictate who you are. Learn how to set your own expectations and they will naturally be forced to view you as an individual with a will and a mind of his own. You must make them realize that you can be trusted to determine success in your own way.

Habit 3: Quit Being Around the Same People

Take a pen and paper and write down the names of the people who surround you, then review them one after the other and ask yourself the following questions:

Do they add value to you and help you or do they pull you down and hurt you?

Do they make you a better person by challenging you to become better or Do they help you take care of/settle tough situations?

Do you gain new experiences, learn from them, and get inspired by them?

If you mostly answered no, it's time to start being around a new set of people who can positively impact your life, inspire you, challenge you, and give you knew experiences. Be around people who can show you how to set goals and plan.

If your friends are not helping you, they are hurting you. So, how do you find new like-minded people who can challenge you, inspire you, and add value to your life?

Attend a party that fits your preference as you will meet people that like the same things as you. Attend a seminar about a topic that interests you and you will meet like-minded people at the venue.

Habit 4: Quit Procrastinating

Unlike other bad habits, procrastination steals your time and paralyzes your future without you even being aware of it.

When you procrastinate, you find it difficult to set goals and take the first step, and you look for excuses to find a way to undertake your tasks later.

People who procrastinate always forget that time will never wait for anyone, yet with limited time, they'd rather accomplish an unimportant task than face what they set out to. For example, when you are supposed to file a report or audit an account for your company, you use that time to play video games or use social media.

People who are successful always make the most of the limited time that is available to them because they are focused and know how to prioritize and set goals. These kinds of people will only engage in habits that will keep them in a state of continuous growth and increased productivity.

Habit 5: Quit Dwelling on Past Failures

Eric H. Mennell

There can hardly be any success story with tasting the sour taste of failure. The ability to rise above failure or disappointment is what defines you as a fighter who deserves to be successful.

When you fail or make mistakes, it is fine to blame yourself a little; however, when you continuously sink into self-blame and self-pity, it does you more harm than good. So, instead of beating yourself up and being a sore loser, you should consider it an opportunity to learn on your journey to success.

Don't destroy yourself for failing; direct that anger towards the failure instead and destroy it. Review your old decisions to find out where you went wrong, why you failed, and what you can do to get a different outcome.

Find a reason to always do it again, change your strategy, adopt a new plan, be flexible, and remain focused and determined that you will get it right if you try it one last time.

Chapter 12:
Forge an Unrelentless Mind and Never Stay Down

Success requires hard work, and the journey to being successful is filled with tough challenges. So, one of the most important tools you will need to succeed is "mental toughness".

When you are confronted with challenges, do you do what it takes to persist and overcome those challenges? Do you do whatever you can to never quit and try one more time every time you fail? When you put determination, willpower, endurance, resilience, and strength all together, in psychology, this is called "mental toughness", and this is what you need to fight your way and struggle through all obstacles to succeed.

When the term mental toughness is mentioned, I would like you to picture athletes who persevere through exhaustion, endure injury, and push themselves to the limit to win - that strength they display is called mental toughness. Another example is a combatant soldier who will grit and endure the fatigue and tired muscles yet will still carry the weight of a wounded comrade on his back to seek medical attention from the battlefield.

Mental toughness has created many superstar gold-winning athletes as well as hero soldiers. The question now is - how do you build mental toughness? How can your tough mental attitude fit into all aspects of your life and help you be successful?

Understanding the Essential Components of Mental Toughness

Mental toughness doesn't just help make great athletes, as many other successful people all over the world have used mental toughness, one way or the other. Before you start building and developing these qualities, you should first know what makes mentally strong people different from others.

Although it might have originated from sports and the military, defining the ability to endure, persevere, remain confident, and stay strong and competitive, it is also now widely used in different fields, and people can now build and develop these qualities to handle difficulties in life.

It helps people in different circumstances effectively deal with changing situations, challenges, pressure, and even factors that might cause stress.

There are 4 key components to these personality qualities:

Control. Puts you in charge and keeps you from losing control to others. You are the controller of every action you take, including your emotions. Your ability to handle, manage and respond to situations is one of your main abilities. You have a firm belief that your destiny and life are fully under your control.

- Challenge: Challenges are viewed as opportunities rather than obstacles.

- Commitment: The ability to undertake tasks until the very end.

- Confidence: Having an unshakable self-belief in your capabilities and ability to be successful.

Qualities of mental toughness can be acquired, trained and developed to fit into various areas of your life and enable you to become successful. To become a mentally tough person, it requires training and consistency.

Positive Self-Talk

SEALs and Athletes all utilize positive talks, especially before, during, and after a mission. The words that you say need to be said in a positive light. It has been estimated that in a minute, you say about 300 – 1000 words to yourself. This is because your brain is a complex part of your body that is always running, and it keeps track of everything you say or do.

When it comes to world-renowned athletes, they believe there is nothing negative in their ways and all they must do is give it their absolute best.

What about SEALs - what method do they employ? Well, they use similar methods; however, theirs are way scarier and can even be considered terrifying.

Imagine yourself underwater with your breathing gear, and without expecting it, your gear is snatched from your mouth, and the oxygen lines are tied into a knot, leaving you to figure out what to do.

The first thing your brain will do is send an alarm, telling you that "you are going to choke to death." However, what you need to do is stay calm while you are underwater and follow the procedure to untie the knot and breathe again.

Your brain starts screaming, "YOU ARE GOING TO DIE." But you must keep cool, stay underwater, and follow the procedure to get your gear working so you can breathe again.

The dangerous part of this drill is panic. For SEALs, panicking is not allowed, so even when they are not able to breathe, they must maintain a clear and calm head.

How can you relate to this and apply it in other fields of your life? I'm sure you have figured it out by now.

The idea is that no matter the obstacle you are facing, if you have a big project or a complex presentation, you are not allowed to panic.

Stay calm and think positive. Remember that you are durable and can outlast any problem, so you just must think.

A pessimist (a loser) will immediately hit the panic button, believing bad situations will last for a very long time or even forever and will say: "There is no way that I can ever get this done." Or, "I am bad at handling this type of thing, I can't do it, and it is not my fault".

An optimist (a winner) will view the obstacles or setbacks in a different way because they have a strong belief that bad things are just temporary and will say: "That sort of thing occasionally happens, but it's no big deal." Or "I know it is not my fault, I am usually good at handling such things, but today was just not my day."

Building mental toughness always requires you to talk positively to yourself and to always remain optimistic.

Build an Unshakable Belief in Your Ability to Achieve Your Goals
When it comes to success, one thing most gold-winning athletes have in common is an "unshakable self-belief".

People with a tough mental attitude don't just think they might win or succeed; they strongly believe that they will. A warrior will never go out thinking that he might succeed; he has the mindset that he will succeed and return to his family and loved ones. When you apply these concepts to other fields of your life, you will get positive results.

Whether you are planning to run a marathon race, shed some weight, quit a bad habit, or do better on a pending task, believe in yourself and tell yourself that you can do it. Be self-encouraging, avoid any form of negative talks and self-doubt, stay positive, and be prepared to carry out what you set your mind to all the way to the end.

Practice Visualization

Close your eyes, relax your mind, and picture a big challenge. Now, imagine yourself as you walk through the challenges step by step. This is a strategy that even the best Olympians and SEALs use. They play it in their mind and watch themselves do it repeatedly.

Athletes are trained daily to develop their imagery skills. They use this method of imagery to get themselves prepared to achieve what they want from their training session. They perfect different skills with imagination, make technical corrections before the actual training commences, and are even able to visualize themselves winning the competition and achieving their goals.

SEALs are also trained and thought to do the same thing; they undergo mental rehearsals where they are taught the techniques to visualize themselves succeeding in a given task, and they are required to go through the steps through visualization.

When SEALs have an important mission, they spend hours every day visualizing any possible error or problem they might encounter during the mission and counter it by creating a visual solution. They go over many scenarios and different possibilities and fix them. They visualize things like a wrong drop zone, a sudden appearance of enemy troops and other problems and emergencies.

How Do You Apply This Strategy?

You need to open your mind, close your eyes and visualize the task that you have before you. Don't just start a fantasy and fantasize that everything is alright and perfect and make yourself feel good about it. This will kill your drive and motivation.

Positive fantasy can cause poor performances and fewer achievements, and the reason is that people can get carried away by the fantasy of visualizing a perfect goal, and at the end of the day, they don't have enough energy to physically pursue their desired goal.

Visualization is aimed to enable you to see the possible problems that you might face and visualize how to solve them.

Now that you are at the stage of visualizing how your big day will be like; you can walk through it step by step to see how you will handle any possible problem.

Use Simulations

The visualization technique is awesome; you can practice it as many times as you want, and you can do it anywhere you are comfortable. However, at the end of it all, you need to also practice hard because practicing is the physical simulation of the real deal.

All medal-winning athletes around the world make use of simulation training extensively. They practice over and over to the point where they breakdown from physical exhaustion and fatigue. They practice as if they were already at the competition, and even wear what they would the day of the actual competition, as well as undergo routines and preparations that they would on the main day.

How Do You Apply This Strategy?

If you have been preparing for a presentation that requires you to stand in front of a large crowd, how are you going to deal with the fear and anxiety that comes with it?

If you are an introvert, or you are just not used to making presentations in front of a crowd, you can use simulation as well. Start by practicing in front of your mirror, then in front of small groups. You can also make use of a supportive group and rehearse in front of them. From there, you can evaluate yourself and find out where you are lacking and how to fix this.

SEALs and athletes are the best at doing their jobs, and we can use the same methods as them to succeed and get results through preparation and hard work.

Conclusion

This journey has been amazing, and we hope that by now, you've been able to gather more than just a few things about exploring the chances that are within you to be whoever you want to be. The mind is like the sky, wide enough for you to explore as much as you are willing to, without a barrier. While flying, the possible obstacles that you may encounter are only physical and like a bird, you may either choose to fly above them or go below. Whatever the case may be, it is essential to eliminate every possibility of quitting. Always tell yourself that it is possible.

If a person can go through a thing as severe as the Navy SEAL training, what can't you do? It's all in your mind, and the most significant barriers are those you have created yourself. What makes you succeed at a task that others have failed is your perspective; if you choose to see the positive side of everything, you will excel even beyond your imagination. It is important to note that everything you are is as a result of your interaction with the world. If you seem to be failing where others are excelling, it is not because failure is part of your DNA, but because you have not acquired the necessary skills to excel. You came to the world as a blank slate, so make conscious efforts to infuse positive things into yourself all the time.

Make sure that with every day that passes, you have taken steps to be better than the previous day. Life is a continuous process of self-development, so never stop working on yourself until the day you die. At the end of it all, everyone dies, but not everyone gets the chance to live, so before you die, make sure you have lived.

If you find this book helpful in anyway a review to support my endeavors is much appreciated.

Relentless and Unbeatable

Eric H. Mennell

www.ingramcontent.com/pod-product-compliance
Lightning Source LLC
Chambersburg PA
CBHW060453080526
44584CB00015B/1428